A TALE OF TWO TALK SHOW HOSTS

ON THE AIR WITH GLENN BECK

Vinnie Penn

Foreword by **GLENN BECK**

Regnery books may be purchased in bulk at special discounts for sales promotion, corporate gifts, fund-raising, or educational purposes. Special editions can also be created to specifications. For details, contact the Special Sales Department, Regnery, 307 Fifth Avenue, 4th Floor, New York, NY 10016 or info@skyhorsepublishing.com.

Regnery® is an imprint of Skyhorse Publishing, Inc.®, a Delaware corporation.

Visit our website at www.regnery.com.
Please follow our publisher Tony Lyons on Instagram @tonylyonsisuncertain.

10 9 8 7 6 5 4 3 2 1

Library of Congress Cataloging-in-Publication Data is available on file.

Cover design by David Ter-Avanesyan
Cover image by Vinnie Penn

Print ISBN: 978-1-5107-8652-3
Ebook ISBN: 978-1-5107-8653-0

Printed in the United States of America

FOREWORD

If I were a wiser man, I'd begin this foreword by assuring you that what you're about to read is pure fiction. Unfortunately, when it comes to Vinnie Penn, nothing is ever *pure*. So instead, let me just say this: I read this book with one eye open, the way you might watch a slow-motion replay of a car crash—especially if the car is *your life*.

Vinnie and I met back in the 1990s, a time when my life was imploding, rebooting, and eventually being redeemed by faith, the love of God, and an extraordinary woman. Much of what he writes may be true . . . but because Vinnie nicknamed me "Oblivio" (for my talent at being utterly oblivious to almost everything—especially women, dating, and basic human interaction), I can't fully confirm any of it. Some of the stories in here I actually discovered for the first time while reading the book—which makes this as educational for me as it is for you.

There was a lot happening in my life during those years. Everything was changing, and Vinnie—in his loud, hilarious, unpredictable way—played a much bigger role in it than I realized then. After finishing the book, I called him and we laughed. A lot. I had forgotten just how many good friends I was blessed with during that season—especially in the city of my rebirth: New

Haven, Connecticut. That city will always belong to Vinnie. I was merely renting space in his kingdom.

I was also reminded—sometimes painfully—of the ways I failed people back then. Notice I said *some* people. Vinnie is not one of my regrets . . . well, at least not completely. I knew early on he had raw talent and a bright future. That talent is on full display here. I was reminded of what I thought back then: "Man, this kid can write." I could see that sure, what I didn't fully grasp was the struggle inside him—just as he couldn't see mine. In the end, that struggle took us to the one thing that is the most important in life that perhaps neither of us knew at the time. Family. It's funny how life turns out: two guys who had no idea how to be husbands or fathers, now counting those as our greatest achievements.

Vinnie tells a story in here about a dinner at Gerry's restaurant after my father-in-law passed away. There we were—three young men, full of dreams, none of which anyone else could really see. Somehow, each of us managed to do more than we ever imagined. That's America. Messy. Redemptive. Amazing.

But the moment that really got me wasn't about career or success. It was watching Vinnie talk with my son—seeing the good, decent, honorable, funny, smart *father* he'd become. I never thought I'd say this, but Vinnie Penn has grown into the kind of man I'd be thrilled to see my son grow into.

I just hope he can do it without the debauchery . . . and the broken-down Camaro.

Enjoy the book. And remember: If anything in here shocks you, imagine how *I* felt reading it.

— Glenn Beck

PREFACE

It should be noted, before we even begin, that I had no idea morning radio shows existed prior to 1996. Not really anyway. I mean, sure, I knew of Casey Kasem and Wolfman Jack, groundbreakers in an industry heretofore unknown to me in all of the ways that would ultimately matter. Cultural icons were popping up doing cameos in the sitcoms of my youth, with the former furthermore on my television every Saturday, counting down the ten biggest songs in the country before imploring me, and a whole damn nation, to "keep your feet on the ground and keep reaching for the stars."

But, zany morning radio shows? "Zoos," as they were known? Where the hosts created all of these kooky, eccentric characters and made appearances at car dealerships and gave away T-shirts and bumper stickers bearing their names? At twenty-nine, it was totally lost on me.

It is important that I get this out of the way before I proceed with the story of my falling into radio and becoming radio superstar Glenn Beck's co-host for three full years—his final years doing Top 40 after close to two decades—lest my naivete and general cluelessness from 1997–1999, about a world that I've now inhabited *since* 1996, come across as either facetious or frustrating. Or both. At the very least, unfathomable.

But, such was the case. I was a cassette kid of the '80s. Prior to that, I was the youngest of four in a family of six where the only thing we listened to in the car was *eight*. As in 8-tracks. My parents didn't dig on local radio and therefore raised four children who didn't. We had a smattering of 8-tracks to choose from, including Sinatra, Elvis, and The Beatles. They were all three in an A rotation.

Sure, there was the local AM station, 1300 WAVZ, that I monitored for snow days, shoveling Cookie Crisp into my face as I eagerly anticipated the host saying "Saint Bernadette School in New Haven" . . . (it took *forever*) . . . "canceled." Now, that was my idea of cancel culture!

And, yes, I became aware of one radio team in town by the time high school rolled around, only because it was where all the new rock music would debut. Word would ramble down the hallowed halls that Zany & McCoy, or Chico & The Boner, or Flash & The Pan (morning radio teams, it appeared, always had wild and woolly names like this) would be giving the newest Def Leppard or Van Halen song a spin at a certain time on a certain day, and either we all tried to be in our cars to catch it, or we had someone who was home taping it on their mammoth bedroom stereo or boom box for us to listen to together later. Until the spring of 1996, I probably, if asked, believed that to be the job: Announce the music, play the music, car commercial, repeat. Lost cause, to be sure, but I had, at the very least, watched *WKRP In Cincinnati*.

This being the case, when I began appearing on *The Glenn Beck Morning Show* sometime that year, I was pleasantly surprised to discover there was a whole lot more to it than that. Sure, Beck played the new music of the day (it was a Top 40 station, after all, but in the late '90s that actually included a solid dose of rock), and he had recurring characters of his creation that made "appearances," but he also waxed philosophical, covered local politics, weighed in on stories of the day—to the point of total digression, where he'd often arrive at the most probing of questions (especially for, say, 6:20 a.m.), leading the phone lines to get lit up by listeners, many of whom were equally prepared to bare their souls.

He'd often crescendo with a sprawling monologue, pausing in their eighth month of pregnancy, woebegone sighs flying, dramatically trailing off at the end as if having lost his way or, worse, seeing a pointlessness to it all, before either making a self-deprecating joke and going to commercials, or apologizing softly for the self-indulgence and going to commercials.

It was captivating. It was compelling. It could have you laughing riotously and taking some serious inventory in the span of five minutes.

I'd been missing out on one hell of a world. As a wannabe writer of fiction and by then a twenty-nine-year-old grappling with pretentiousness as much as I was the fact that thirty was barreling toward me and I was absolutely, positively nowhere, the self-flagellation went into fourth gear for not even knowing this kind of entertainment was taking place all around me, these types of opportunities not a two-hour train ride to New York City away, but fifteen minutes *by car*.

It didn't take me long to realize that I wanted in. *This* was what everyone was doing on FM morning radio? Sketches and monologues and conversations with complete strangers on the phone that could be as quippy as they were contemplative?

No. It was not what everyone was doing. It's what Glenn Beck was doing. It was the fusion of entertainment and enlightenment.

CHAPTER ONE

WANNABE

It was the best of times, it was the worst of times. From 1997–2000 the former was surely the case for me, while the latter was where Glenn Beck whiled away many an hour.

I first met him in the hallway of Radio Towers Park in Hamden, Connecticut, which houses a handful of radio stations. It was by chance one afternoon in 1996. Except it wasn't by chance at all. It was planned out. Choreographed. Staged. I just didn't know that. And wouldn't know that for over a quarter of a century.

By then Glenn was in his fifth year doing mornings for heritage New Haven Top 40 station KC101. Many big names in the industry have passed through the very same doors for a stint, including Radio Hall of Famer Kid Kelly and Tom Poleman, a programming veteran who is now president of iHeartRadio, to name just two.

Beck's Top 40 partner Pat Gray had come with him to New Haven, by way of Baltimore and a few other much more significant markets (New Haven wasn't—and isn't—even in the Top 100 of radio markets) but had long since returned to the other side of the country, and Beck was struggling to find a replacement co-host. He'd done a year with a female co-host but deemed that a disaster, and now simply had the studio basically full of bodies with standard-issue radio nom de plumes, from the "news guy" to the "weather girl" to the "traffic person" to even a production guy and—oh yeah—a chef. (The chef was not there to prepare meals, by the way; he was just a guy who'd catered many a KC101 event and Beck found him amusing, so why not throw him in the mix too?) They might've been calling it "The Breakfast Flakes" or something equally appalling, but not to the point of changing any logos or banners to reflect that. Heaven forbid a billboard! Those were, and are, sacred. In other words, Beck wasn't sold on this motley crew. Nor was management.

Lemme back up a second and add a little more water to the story of the chef. Because, doesn't it kinda beg for it? He was short-lived on the show, but my mention of him should by no means be viewed as some illustration of how desperate Beck and management were. I mean, they were desperate (again, I'd find out just how desperate more than twenty-five years later), but it's not like the FedEx guy could drop off a package, launch a zinger that reduced Beck to tears, and find himself co-hosting the next day. (Although the FedEx guy during our time together, I once remarked, "looked like Santa" and sure as hell became a regular on the show; he wound up being a biker who held an annual toy drive where he played—you guys are so good!—Santa Claus.)

This chef was carving a path for himself as a media personality in addition to his culinary strides. At one point a wildly successful caterer who lived less than ten minutes from the radio station, he was also doing regular appearances on *The Today Show*. At another time he was the Senior Executive Chef of Sara Lee (a $20 billion dollar behemoth in the food world in the days before the term "foodie" even existed, never mind "food porn") and—I'm not kidding here—doing regular appearances on *The Tony Danza Show*. Yep. *That* kind of big time.

An affable, lovable lug, he brought a lot of energy and charisma to any set. Why wouldn't that also be the case if instead of a set it were a radio station? Beck was as sold on him being given a shot as KC101's General Manager was, and so another ingredient got tossed into the pot.

This was not just the beauty of both Beck and his then-General Manager, a woman named Faith Zila, who actively sought Glenn out and lured him to New Haven in the first place. It was also something that happened in radio a lot in those days: Be funny, get on the air. Stay funny, stay on the air. Background notwithstanding.

I should know. It was about to happen to me.

Zila and Beck were a match made in heaven. More than Beck and Gray. More than Beck and me. Where she was a free spirit, he was a free thinker. They both thought outside the box in their respective roles in what was at the time a thriving industry. They both had incredible work ethics. They both abhorred the cookie-cutter approach, much more keen on throwing things at the wall to see what would stick. The types of things that pretty much everyone else in the industry would warn might take your eye out.

Faith came from the world of sales, had risen through the ranks to GM, and was as Bohemian as the day is long. She wore long, flowing numbers—a la Mrs. Roper from TV's *Three's Company*—every last one of them black, and there was a touch of goth to her look too, during a time when goth was king. She was most certainly queen of radio in Connecticut, though she'd surely bristle the mere suggestion. She held her own in boardrooms full of men, oftentimes leaving them trembling in her wake. What she wanted, she got. She wanted Beck, and she got him. She wanted me; she got me. I just didn't know she wanted me at the time.

Faith Zila changed both my life and Beck's.

I set up an interview with her through—shocker of all shockers—a local car dealership. A childhood friend of mine was in his car salesman era, and he'd been harping for ages that I "should be a DJ," thanks to rants I'd go on about music, typically with a drink in my hand by the blazes of a bonfire in his backyard (long before the age of firepits). He'd always profess to be in awe of my knowledge about members of bands, producers of certain records, the years they were released. He thought me an encyclopedia. I explained to him time and again that DJs had to have a technical prowess, a mastering of this goliath board before them, along with an ability to rhythmically conjoin songs with patter, all while thrusting knobs up and down. "They don't just sit there and talk about music for twenty minutes," I'd laughingly admonish the idiot. (The idiot, again, lest you already forgot, we'd discover was me.)

This had actually begun years back, but now he was working at a car dealership that advertised on KC101. He had somehow finagled Faith Zila's card from someone there and passed it on to me. "Call her up and set up an interview. You never know" was his logic.

And, nope. You sure as shit don't.

I don't know what made me call, but I did. My stomach growling? Overdue utility bills? The fact that I was paying for gas with coins? And she took the meeting. Now, I wasn't calling to be a "DJ." My thought process was that I could write copy for the radio station's brand spanking new website. They were "the latest thing" in 1996, though in their very, *very* early stages, and my thought was that I could bring something to that table. See, at the time, I was a freelance writer for the area's newspapers, covering the music scene. I'd interview bands that were coming to town and write up articles about it. I was going to lead with my latest: I had just interviewed Jakob Dylan, son of Bob, and front man for the band The Wallflowers. Their hit "One Headlight" was getting played every twenty minutes on KC101.

But it's not like I told the receptionist any of this. Or Faith. She'd never even gotten on the phone. She knew nothing of my master plan. I merely dropped the car dealership's name, and mine, to the receptionist, got put on hold, and when she came back on the line she said, "Faith will see you." Like The Great Oz. My goal was to get her on the phone. Now I had to show up. Presumably in a tie. Which I didn't have. Get Dad on the phone.

When the day came for my interview for a job that didn't even exist (yet did, although I wouldn't know it did until—are you still playing?—over twenty-five years later), I was ushered into her office, which was a sight to behold. There was a chandelier. Leather furniture like you were in a cigar shoppe. She came from around her desk to greet me and took a seat on one of the couches, and I took a seat on the other, immediately launching into everything my college professors prompted me to do, along with some additional tips from a mother who had gotten so exhausted by my freeloading throughout my twenties she moved across the country with her second husband, to Vegas. She left my sister and me in the family house, where we were instructed to simply keep it going.

Faith sat there beaming as I went on and on (and on) about all that I could offer to a website that I might not have even taken a look at. My legitimate thought process was, "I'll give you the interviews that I'm conducting of all the artists you're playing on the air that I turn into articles for several local newspapers and 'zines and you can post them on the site." I was utterly clueless to the fact that the newspapers owned those. They were not mine to sell a *second time*. Hence, this wouldn't even be possible. In my defense, I was also offering my services to conduct interviews and do write-ups specifically for the website, otherwise unpublished, as my Rolodex had grown considerably in the half dozen years since I scored my first byline. I truly had already scored interviews with some of the biggest (or soon-to-be) 1990s names: Counting Crows, Bush, Alanis, Collective Soul, No Doubt, one of Blind Melon lead singer Shannon Hoon's final interviews, and more. I eagerly, albeit clumsily, yanked them one by one from my briefcase and held them up to show Faith. It was the saddest show-and-tell starring a twenty-nine-year-old man.

I needn't have bothered. She was sold on me the minute I opened my mouth. I've no idea why. She just sat there, beaming. I can still see it to this day. She never "heard" my pitch, and therefore I was never called on to deliver on the website front. She politely allowed me to finish and then just simply said, "Well, I love you. I think you should be on the air."

And so I was. That weekend.

Somewhere in the melee of introductions that followed, all Glenn-free, I heard one programmer mention to another the words "lifestyle reporter" while they were talking about me. *What the hell is that and how am I qualified to be one?*

In retrospect, it all seems so obvious, as most things do in retrospect. But at the time I was just a fumbling and bumbling freelance writer, pitching stories to a variety of different publications on a weekly basis—from national rock mags to lifestyles publications like *GQ* and *Esquire* to a newly resurrected *Spy Magazine* (man, I wanted in on that one) to iconic comedic pubs like *MAD Magazine* and *Cracked* to each and every local player, from the artsy rags one could grab for free at a coffee shoppe across the street from Yale to every newspaper, including the *Hartford Courant*, which, to this day, remains the longest-running newspaper still in print in America.

The no's came fast and furious, and that's when I'd get any response at all. Rejections were plentiful, while three squares a day were not. Such is the life. You know it going in.

But there were enough yeses slowly beginning to trickle in, on a quasi-steady basis, after nearly ten years at it. (Another frequent target of mine: Marvel Comic Books. Their process was *incredibly* streamlined. It got to the point where I'd mail my latest pitch for an issue of a barely there title on a Monday and receive their letter back that it was a pass the very next Monday. But I was getting to them. Their form letter began having handwritten notes in the upper right-hand corner, and they were getting more and more detailed.)

But I digress. Which I may do a lot. Sorry in advance.

Point is, I had a steady enough stream of income by this point, and I felt like I finally might actually be getting somewhere, so the fact that there was no formal job offer, job title, or even a mention of salary, did not make me so much as arch an eyebrow. This was just more freelancing.

I figured that I'd write a script and deliver it into a microphone as opposed to typing it up on the typewriter I was beating the hell out of, where the *n* was broken. (You know how many words contain that letter? *So* many! I just used one there! And there! You know how laborious it is to turn *every m* into an *n* with a thin black marker before faxing your latest piece over? It was the stuff of carpal tunnel.)

The artist, he sure does starve. But, again, like I say, I was slowly beginning to eat. Okay, *snack*.

It never dawned on me to ask any questions. Like, why do you want *me* to do this? I showed you a writing portfolio beneath that chandelier. Or, you've got three studios full of on-air talent—can't any one of them do this sixty second spot about a Potato & Corn Festival in North Branford? What's more, I wasn't excited about any of it either. Later, I'd watch as people got so excited at the prospects of being on the radio, but, curiously, I did not go through that at the time. Or ever.

I was neither excited nor nervous. I just had one eye on thirty and the other on my bank account.

Sometimes they'd want me on the scene, there in the thick of it all, very "man on the street." This would necessitate me finding a pay phone to call in to the radio station so someone could roll tape on me among all the chaos of the festival or parade attendees, which could occasionally prove quite the challenge. Pay phones were on their way out and cell phones on their way in, and I'd occasionally find myself quite literally running blocks from an event to locate a phone to plunk my coin into. Then it dawned on me that no one knew if I was truly there or not, so I just began making these calls from my front porch at home. Where you could hear a pin drop. Or, worse, hear a random lone bark from my dog. He was starving too.

"Hey, it's Vinnie Penn LIVE from the forty-seventh annual New Haven Chili Fest! Somebody grab me a water—this stuff is H-O-T hot!" That kinda thing.

But, other times it'd be in studio, even frequenting one of the local morning shows in the building, on 960-WELI. The host could count on me for a solid punch line every time out but, more importantly, I knew all the ins and outs of the city that I was born and raised in. The street names and popular clubs, from the old to the new, and the concert venues, and the theaters. The names came out of my mouth with as much ease as my three siblings' names. That mattered. No retrospect necessary. I saw this then.

But what I didn't see was the grooming. I was being prepped to get thrown in with Beck.

One chilly autumn day, on my way out of the WELI studio, I ran into him in the hallway, strolling in my direction with the program director (heretofore referred to as the PD), an Italian guy from Rhode Island. (Except for the fact that I didn't run into him at all; it'd been choreographed, I would find out over drinks with someone I'd come to work with there some twenty-five years later, her disbelief that I never knew this making martini shoot out her nose.)

I was introduced to Glenn, who was taken by the wool cap that sat atop my head. It was a Yale hat, with the legendary Ivy League institution's inimitable "Y" going solo on it, no bulldog to be found.

After a very softspoken hello, he asked me if I'd "been through Yale." My response was that I surely had, sardonically adding "in my car." Mildly entertained, we shook hands, and the wildest of lightbulbs went off over the PD's head. "Hey!" he blurted out. "You should pop in on Glenn one morning. I am just now coming up with this idea. This is most definitely not something that the GM instructed me to coordinate, nor did I plan it that Glenn and I would be walking by the studio just as you were walking by it." He turned to Glenn. "Vinnie's really funny."

I am fairly certain that the guy hadn't listened to me on-air one single time—especially over in the wasteland that was the lowly AM news/talk station, as opposed to the "50-watt blowtorch" (radio folk *love* to use that term) that was the FM Top 40 juggernaut known as KC101.

So, was it that lame Yale crack? That was just a zippy reply. The stuff of icebreaker. After all, Beck didn't appear all that enthusiastic about introductions to the guy faking festival appearances on the tiny news/talk station in the building, getting paid chump change. Heck, a few times they even paid me with gift certificates. At least they were to restaurants, so I could eat.

He was certainly gentlemanly enough. And his reaction to my wisecrack was sincere. But he appeared very much the weary traveler. He shrugged his shoulders affably and said "sure" to the PD, who I'd in short order discover Beck thought a complete fool.

For the life of me, the first time I was in-studio I can't remember a single thing about what we discussed or any jokes I might've made that landed. And, in the end, that's why I was in there: To be funny. That much had been made clear. There was an ease, though. An immediate comfort and smooth rapport. Armed with a good night's sleep, I brought zero awkwardness or nervousness into that studio. Radio hosts are so grateful for that, despite it totally not being under anyone's control. Still, those jittery, sweat-stained, "talk into the mic, *INTO* the mic" guests only ratchet up the host's nervousness and are ultimately just so draining.

What I do recall, I can tell you, is that it was later that very week, on a Thursday, and in between 7:30 and 8:00 a.m. It would be eons before I'd find out what prime real estate that is on a morning radio show, what a coveted slot.

Land they must have, because once I was done Beck not only asked me to return the following Tuesday, but he gave me an assignment. Moreover, a topic. I didn't think much of it at the time, if anything at all, but by God the assignment was so telling of where Beck was at, where he was headed, and, perhaps most important of all, where KC101 did not want to be or go or, heaven forbid, stay.

Beck told me to prepare a monologue about incumbent Bill Clinton seeking reelection up against stone-faced Bob Dole and wild card Ross Perot.

During those early visits I'd handwrite my bits on notebook paper, tear 'em out after one final pass in the parking lot, jutting lines through words and writing punchier ones atop the mess, and head into the building without so much as performing it out loud once. They looked like the sleeve to Pearl Jam records.

The gist of this particular bit was "*this* is the best America can do?" (A till I still revisit, tragically, often.) I likened each candidate to a TV series, and can only recall my Bob Dole slam, which elicited the biggest laugh from Beck. I said he was the *Murder One* of the lot, a nod to an ABC series that was limping along in its second and, ultimately, final season. It was something along the lines of "and Dole is 'Murder One.' It's like, is this still even on the air?"

I was asked back again for that Thursday and given another assignment. But this one wasn't a topic; It was a "sign-off." He wanted me to come up with a way to end each of my monologues, tie it all up in a pretty li'l bow, going so far as to instruct me to come up with a few and that he'd pick his favorite.

When I returned two days later, I rattled off everything that I'd come up with. I don't recall any of them and, if I'm being honest, I'm pretty sure I wasn't even all that clear on what he was asking me to do. It would later spark one of the first of our hours-long conversations, this one being about comedy legends, classic films, literature, and so forth. We discovered we shared a love for Abbott and Costello and other old, "black and white" fare. These TV and radio forefathers all had their sign-offs and catch phrases and recitable routines.

After I bounced my final idea off Beck about how I'd end my segments going forward, he deadpanned, "OK, so *those* all suck." Then he chortled. Yet he wasn't joking; he hated them all. The first thing I truly—and I do mean truly—noticed about Glenn Beck was that his laughter was contagious. It still is. I burst out laughing in that moment, too. I would soon notice he also used it to great effect on the air. Not that he'd ever fake laugh—he just laughed in a way that goaded someone less inclined to join right on in. His laugh when we were alone, out at the movies we'd soon be frequenting, or at his apartment for one of his legendary dinner parties, was the same as the one you'd get in the studio, but that one went directly into the microphone, or began slightly away from the microphone, only to move toward it as it got heavier, or the other way around. He played that microphone like a goddamn banjo.

With less than a minute before I was to go live on the air—and it was *all* live pretty much *all* the time—Beck had his eyes on the clock and was spinning those dials and working those nobs like Doctor Frankenstein as the storm neared. The multitasking was insane, a far cry from the way radio is done today. Entire shows are taped in advance and timed to go off hours later. There ain't even a body in the studio.

The song playing was nearing its end, and I already knew what Glenn turning his microphone on looked like, and he was just about to do it. *It's alive! A-live!* He glanced at me and spat out, "When you're done, just say 'I'm Vinnie Penn, but that's my problem.'"

Monster born.

I became a regular on The Glenn Beck Morning Show, going live every Tuesday and Thursday at 7:35 a.m. I'd punctuate every rant with "I'm Vinnie Penn, but that's my problem," and sure enough people began calling in, eager to say it right on back to me. They especially loved saying it to my face, once I began popping in on Glenn's appearances at area grocery stores, diners, and—oh yeah, most of all—car dealerships. Aka the radio shows of the 70s and 80s' bread and butter.

As early as my third or fourth time doing my bit, Beck revealed another card up his estimable sleeve: my introduction. The first few times he'd simply say "Vinnie Penn is in with us again. What's hacking you off this week, Vinnie?" And away I'd go. I recall giving pause the first time he used the term "hacking you off." That was not vernacular indicative of the region. That was something he brought with him from Mount Vernon. Or maybe picked up during his time in Baltimore. I felt like it really made him stick out like a sore thumb, like *so not a local*. Hence, the quest for a me.

But the brevity that gave way to the levity was dropped extraordinarily early on. Suddenly there came this epic introduction, complete with dramatic F/X humming beneath Beck's polished delivery. "He writes for *MAD* magazine and *Circus*. His work has also appeared in *Spy* magazine (it had not) and *Hit Parader*, and he joins us live in-studio every Tuesday and Thursday at this time. Vinnie Penn. How's it going, Vinnie?"

I was also no longer assigned topics. I was to come up with them myself and Beck would either cue up a song that worked with what I'd be talking about on a given day or I was to also have that worked out. One time my segment was going to be about a recurring dream I was having and why dreams needed to recur at all. After Beck's intro he cued up the opening strains to Aerosmith's classic "Dream On," and I was off. He'd fade it out once I got going, but by the time I delivered my "I'm Vinnie Penn, but that's my problem" outro he slammed into that right hook final chorus, where Steven Tyler's plea for the listener to dream on becomes a guttural, shrieking battle cry, Joe Perry's guitar squeal begging for sunroofs to be opened. He'd let the chorus breathe, and then ultimately ride the song right into a commercial stopset.

(Interestingly, Aerosmith was quite active on the Top 40 charts at the time. Their single "Pink," from their Nine Lives record, would earn them a Grammy Award in 1997, and "I Don't Wanna Miss a Thing," off the soundtrack to the Bruce Willis/Ben Affleck flick *Armageddon*, would score the Boston rockers their one and only number one single the next year. That said, we had no business playing "Dream On." That was classic rock. That RI PD was destroying his office when Glenn would plug in my "intro music." But I wouldn't find out about that until a year and a half later, at his farewell party. And, again, Aerosmith was still topping the charts with new material. There were times we used Jim Croce songs or Pink Floyd, the former having been dead for decades and the latter having not spoken to each other in decades.)

Beck was making the segment, and the guy starring in it, both larger than life. It was strategic. Yes, I was getting stuff published regularly in *Hit Parader* and *Circus*, but *MAD* magazine appeared to get turned on by rejecting my work, and *Spy* never so much as dignified a single pitch of mine with a response. Glenn wanted me to seem like a "get." Like a big deal. And since his listeners trusted him, they believed him. Not that he was consciously lying—he didn't commit who I contributed to regularly to memory. But bombast was the key and, as Beck would often acquiesce: "It *is* theater." Within six months I was added to the show full-time, all morning every morning, Monday through Friday.

But this time salary did get brought up.

The night before I was to have my sit-down with RI PD to finalize the details of my contract, Beck called me at home. "Listen," he began softly, from an apartment within walking distance to the radio station that he had only recently moved into while he went through a divorce. "I know exactly how much money they have for this job. If they offer you one penny less than it just say no and—pay attention—just stand your ground. They have the money."

I'd never had a salary before. Despite being twenty-nine years old. It's not pathetic in retrospect; but I was very much aware at the time, and reminded often by all those around me just how pathetic that was. The fact that I was twenty-nine years old and had no medical benefits was an extraordinary bone of contention with my mother, as it would be for any mom. Every few months she'd go on a tear about the fact that I didn't have health insurance, punctuating every tirade with a send-off along the lines of "don't step in front of a bus today" or "don't break your leg falling down a flight of stairs." As if I otherwise might. I'd sometimes counter, "But Ma, the bus could be *so* tempting . . ." We'd always had a funny patter. She'd soon be a recurring guest on the show.

The call from Beck unnerved me. I was fully prepared to accept *whatever* they offered. It was four hours a morning. It wouldn't interfere at all with my freelancing. Plus, it came with those much-ballyhooed medical benefits, no matter how meager the package might be. Sure, the number he told me was chump change. The epitome of a starting salary. Being honest, less than pretty much any starting salary ever offered for any job in the history of man. But I still would've done the job for less.

"Promise me," Glenn kept pressing. "I'm telling you I know exactly how much money they have. You've gotta trust me. I used to be the station manager (which was true, although that was short-lived), so I'm telling you this is what they have. Don't accept any less."

The following day, immediately following the show, I began to make my way over to the PD's office. Much to my surprise, Glenn rushed out of the studio behind me and began walking with me. "Remember what I said," he began. "I know this guy. He's going to offer you less. But I know exactly how much money they've got. You've just gotta turn him down until he gets there. You trust me, don't you?"

Of course I did. Outside of the fact that he'd been working at my hometown radio station, and in this market, for years already, he'd worked at several other radio stations, in several other markets, prior to this stint. He'd been through countless negotiations by this point, including the one he was presently navigating with his wife's lawyer, even though he just turned thirty-three. He'd first begun cashing checks from radio stations as a teenager in Mount Vernon. I was getting gift certificates to Chinese restaurants for my radio work.

When I got to the office, I turned to him and said, "Well, I'll let you know how it goes." Little did I know he'd be sitting in on the meeting, too. The PD didn't even know.

"Can Vinnie and I have a minute alone?" he asked Glenn.

"I won't say a word," was Glenn's response, as he made himself comfortable on the sofa. (In the '90s, program directors for radio stations had beautiful furniture in their office. This was, ostensibly, to make the record label folk comfortable, but the fact that it was nicer than anything in any of the DJ's homes oftentimes stung. So we'd get them back by having sex on it all the time.)

These two were staring each other down like it was the Old West. "What are you, his babysitter?" Glenn was asked. He softly reiterated: "I won't say a word." The guy was *ticked*, but Glenn didn't flinch.

We were in there no more than two minutes. True to his word, Glenn never made a peep. I was offered five thousand dollars per year less than the figure Beck had shared with me. I immediately accepted.

On our way back down the hall—a walk of shame like no other, and years before the catch phrase would even first be uttered—Glenn put his arm around me and cooed into my ear, "You're a tower of Jell-O."

After the next day's show, I went to sign the contract that had since been drawn up. I'd be signing it with Faith, who was beaming yet again, and Glenn joined me for that, too.

"This is it," she said to him, gripping his arms. I had no idea that a search had been underway, and for a good long time too. Or, at the very least, for long enough that it was starting to wear on Beck. The divorce surely wasn't helping either. Faith was genuinely happy for him, though. I could see in her eyes that she just adored the guy. She'd talked him into slumming it in New Haven, the first time in his career he wasn't working in a market in the Top 100 and, damn it, she was going to keep him happy.

She was genuinely happy for me, too. She gave me a big hug and had tears in her eyes as I signed my first radio contract.

"I heard Glenn went into the meeting with you," she said. I nodded that he had. She turned to him, tilted her head, and pursed her lips, eyes welling up even further. She was well aware that Glenn's intention was to add a pressure to the RI PD. His accompanying me caused the PD to grumble about him yet again afterwards to Faith, which I'd find out about maybe a year later. The PD deemed Beck's joining the tete-a-tete inappropriate, intrusive, disrespectful, and as such deserving of reprimand. He would spend his remaining days at the station in a power struggle with his morning man. One that he'd always lose.

"You two are going to be inseparable," Faith predicted, now one hand gripping Glenn's forearm and the other gripping mine.

And we were. For two years.

CHAPTER TWO

TUBTHUMPING

Glenn's apartment was a dump.

I mean, not the *inside*. The guy had an eye for interior design, his hallway lined with framed photos of either him with a former president of the United States, a historical document, or an autographed picture of him with the likes of B.B. King or Eric Clapton. What hung on the walls in his living room was more of the same, only considerably larger. Each shelf held a piece of history or an eye-catching work of art. For a newly-minted bachelor, he kept his place spotless.

There were two bedrooms, and I recall the one for his two young daughters, Mary and Hannah, looking like something straight out of a ride at Disney. It, too, was spotless and loaded with all the magical trappings of childhood: stuffed animals and topnotch toys, twin beds adorned with comforters that somehow appeared weaved by elves.

Outside the front door to Beck's new(-ish) digs the stench of weed and "Bangladeshian stews" (that was the joke) hung in the air while cursing and shouting and just a general cacophony battered you. Inside managed to make you forget about all of that the second you closed said door behind yourself, candles lit, music playing, his considerable CD collection lining the floorboards of his entire living room, lending itself just enough to a dorm-like quality. Beyond that, there'd be the smell of whatever he happened to be preparing for dinner, which managed to override the . . . um . . . foreign delicacies that otherwise permeated the air of this $550-per-month (or thereabouts) apartment complex where there were always—*always*—several apartments available.

(Oh, and the smallest elevator ever known to man elicited an immediate fear upon entering, and somehow managed to be crooked. It groaned as it lifted you cockeyed to Beck's floor and sighed as it brought you down to the bottom. I can't even get into the laundry room.)

But this was life as Beck knew it now, and those dinners were being made for a handful of guests often, as 1997 was Beck's Dinner Party era. Newly single, in the throes of losing everything in the divorce, his once-popular morning radio show in a state of decline (along with his morale), he sought solace in the company of coworkers and the few good friends he'd made since moving to Connecticut every night he didn't have his daughters.

He struggled with being alone.

As such, I began getting invited there quite often, to the point of it affecting the relationship I'd been in for years. But that had never necessarily been a healthy relationship, and soon Beck would have a wingman for what would wind up being a fairly short period of time as an eligible bachelor. Until then, though, I alone had the privilege of hitting the town with a newly-single and newly-sober Glenn Beck.

We went on several double dates together. This was another small town morning radio show phenomenon previously lost on me: The dating pool sure as hell ain't a kiddie one. This sucker is Olympic. They came out of the woodwork! I was genuinely perplexed when I first realized just how much people viewed the small town local radio host as celebrity. In the late '90s, being an on-air radio personality on the station everyone listens to in your hometown managed to appear the equivalent of being lead singer (or guitarist) in a band that had one hit song some ten years earlier.

This was new to me, but not to Beck. Or, at the very least, it wasn't lost on Beck. After all, he'd married in his early twenties, so how much had he ever truly enjoyed these types of perks that came with the gig? This being the case, he entered every new relationship with a healthy dose of skepticism, and that was mixing in a bowl of the jadedness that comes with divorce.

He'd go on and on about red flags while I went on and on about red thongs.

Still, between taking his daughters to see *Les Mis* on Broadway an astonishing number of times, he managed to enjoy this brief period, this ultimately very short chapter in the book of his life, to the best of his hopeless romantic ability. Further, there was now a guy at his side (me) who he'd repeatedly say he genuinely enjoyed watching experience a world not only heretofore unknown to him, but also one that Beck had managed to fall in love with in middle school, thanks to his portable radio and a patient and charitable local radio host/mentor in *his* small town.

Plus, I babysat! (He has no recollection of this, which I deem a defense mechanism, but his wonderful daughters Mary and Hannah do.)

One night my Chevy Camaro, which had already proven to be a go-to punchline for Beck that listeners just gobbled right up, broke down on my way to his place. After calling a tow truck, he generously offered to loan me his old Volvo to use until my car was repaired. He brought me by the house he'd bought for his wife, where he'd planned to raise his children, and my jaw hit the floorboard upon seeing what he'd left behind to live where he was living now.

It was a beautiful, even historical, do-it-yourselfer owned by a guy who couldn't do a damn thing in it himself. But he could effortlessly charm who *could* do what needed to be done—from a new roof or reinforced front porch—to become a sponsor on his radio show. And in lieu of payment for the commercials Beck did for them live, as opposed to pretaped, and delivered organically with zeal and fluidity, ("weaving it into the storyline of the show"—his words), he'd get the labor. Such deals were commonplace.

Sadly, the marriage was falling apart in lockstep with the house, and Beck was now living in those new digs, around the corner from the radio station—the apartment complex had a huge banner that read No down payment, No security, and they meant it when it came to the security.

His ability to go from wealthy to broke, and from a big, charming New England home oozing character to a glorified dorm room where people were regularly mugged in the parking lot, impressed the hell out of me. Not a lot of people can do that. Beck measured success by how happy you were, if you were passionate about what you were doing, and if you were making a difference while doing it. He didn't measure it by the toys; by the extravagant home and expensive watches and expensive cars. He had the expensive watches, though. But the house was expendable and that Volvo ran like crap.

I absolutely believe Beck could go back to broke even today and adjust accordingly.

It was during these early days of our working together that Beck shared just how close he'd been to quitting not just KC101, but radio entirely. There were two prominent reasons: The first was that the state of flux his show had been in for some time, with its revolving door of auditions disguised as recurring guests, was getting the best of him (i.e., he was not happy with the show, passionate about the show, and didn't feel like he was making a difference with the show), and the second was that he viewed radio as a "dying industry."

The first one had now been resolved, albeit via a band-aid that'd morph into a bridge. I was on board, we genuinely enjoyed each other as people and as coworkers, and the show was being talked about in a way it hadn't been in ages. At least, that's what I was told. Listenership was up. Again, I was told. Attendance at radio station events was wayyy up. Same. Ratings were too. That one, however, could be—and was—confirmed. The show leapt from #3 to #1, according to Arbitron. Immediately.

This was all "just in time" he'd mutter. When I asked him what a guy who'd done radio all his life would do if he quit the business in his nearing mid-thirties, he answered earnestly, "I was thinking about the ministry."

One of the first gals he'd dated briefly at the time reiterated this to me one night, adding that I should feel honored because, thanks to me, he was no longer considering that. His passion for the show had returned. My writing ambitions reignited his for radio.

In true self-deprecating Beck fashion, he laughed heartily at the notion of even the idea of me feeling honored. Then he leaned toward me solemnly, striking a serious tone: "I just felt like I lost something here, ya know? So, I felt I had to leave. I actually still feel like something's missing." I took this sincere admission in for the briefest of moments before hitting him back with, "If you lost something here, the only place you're going to find it is here." He sat back and let that wash over him, taking comfort in the concept, appreciative of the sentiment, exhaling.

The second, however, loomed overhead like a dark cloud, and would for the remainder of our time together. This industry had an expiration date. Of this he was certain. And it was barreling down on us. I abhorred when he'd bring this up. Both because I believed him and because I was falling in love with it.

CHAPTER THREE

IT'S ALL COMING BACK TO ME NOW

The woman waiting for me in the lobby was clearly outside our "target demo," two words that would come to strike fear in my heart over the course of my first few years doing Top 40 radio—it inspired stress, anxiety, and I could often hear myself gulp upon it being said to me, perspiration racing to the surface of my skin.

She was, I'd say, in her late thirties, and here we were spinning the biggest hits of the day, targeting teenyboppers and their older sisters home from college, or maybe just beginning their careers. I spied her through the studio window, which she was *not* positioned in front of, like so many others, just watching while we spoke animatedly, gesticulating and pressing buttons in a way that suggested we were in a bad play where we were playing characters who were launching rockets. Glenn oft-referred to the studio as a "fishbowl" for this very reason—the staring of complete strangers either awaiting an appointment with a salesperson or perhaps picking up a prize they had won by being caller number whatever, their gaze at once intense and distracting. We *were* performing, after all.

She cradled a baby in her arms and waited patiently. Other radio station visitors, I would come to learn, felt as if we could pop out any time we liked, or that they could simply roll on in and hang out like the studio was their bestie's basement. Barbara, the receptionist, had let her in, asked how she could help her, got the words "I'm here to see Vinnie," and buzzed me on the studio line to tell me so. That's it. No "What about?" or "Is he expecting you?" Babs wasn't necessarily inquisitive, and I would many months later come to learn that the mere suggestion of a security guard by the on-air staff would make any and all managers break up, and *out* with hives. The "talent" were full of themselves to suggest something so outlandish and unnecessary! It was also costly and, if reverberated, could unnerve execs higher up.

When I finally got out to the lobby, I extended my hand and immediately realized my faux pas, as she couldn't exactly shake it, what with a baby in her arms.

"You were talking about that old movie theater in town being demolished yesterday on your show," she said, eschewing small talk in favor of getting right to why she was there. I nodded, recalling the story and how I described this outdated two-screen theater that I considered ancient at ten, never mind twenty-nine. Glenn being a transplant, several times over, knew nothing of its history or condition. Again, I was the local, a New Haven lifer who could inject the show with a real knowledge of the city, never mind state, memories swirling 'round my head of seeing Chevy Chase and Goldie Hawn in *Foul Play* there, and being uncomfortable *then*, in the days long before reclining, vibrating, luxury seating. Never mind stereo sound! This theater sounded like it had the same speaker our father would configure onto the rolled-down window of his Ford Falcon when he took us to the drive-in.

"You were saying how uncomfortable the seats in the theater were," she continued. Yes. Funny, huh? I had gone on a nice little tear, got everyone in the studio laughing—from Glenn to the traffic girl, news guy, and even interns. I recall thinking she must have either also found it funny, or maybe had some vested interest in the decaying structure's death sentence.

"You said halfway through any movie there you felt like you had spina bifida." Hah! That's right, I did. None of it written either—off the cuff, on a roll, *in the zone*. So that's why she was here! She cracked up too; probably in her car, on her way to work. And here we were on her day off. Lemme grab that Sharpie for my first ever autograph. "This little man in my hands has spina bifida," she said, sternly, straight-faced, terse. Then she asked me to hold him, foisting him into my arms. My heart raced. He was adorable, she was angry.

It was my fourth day doing morning radio, and seven years before I'd have a child of my own.

As much as admonishment like that could—and should—absolutely pulverize you, Glenn was quick with the showbiz quotes when it came, as was one of our engineers. That engineer said "the show must go on" to me more times than I can count in my first year, and I needed to hear it every time. Beck was big on the show being the equivalent of theater, and "getting them to feel something—anything," etc.

I vividly recall a day, fairly early on, several months before I'd even been offered a permanent place on the show, when I listened as Glenn took a call from a listener some ten minutes or so after I'd finished my twice-weekly "spot." She probably thought I was long gone by then, but I kinda doubt she'd care if I was or not. Callers were the original keyboard warriors.

She told Glenn in no uncertain terms that she was not a fan "of this Vinnie guy" and that I was "too sarcastic." Up until that point I'd only gotten positive feedback (again, this was before the baby with spina bifida, and that woman was more interested in me becoming educated than she was angry with me), so I was taken aback and, surprisingly, it even stung. I say surprisingly because it's not like I hadn't been criticized or insulted before. I grew up in a neighborhood where the blows were low, even when delivered by friends. Especially when delivered by friends. Plus, I could wallpaper my room, and my sister's, with the aforementioned, oftentimes vicious rejection letters I'd gotten from everyone from Archie Comics to *GQ*.

Glenn couldn't believe I gave such a shit. Especially because so many listeners had already been calling in to gush, and even flirt. Lotsa flirting.

He laughed initially but then saw that considerable wind had been taken out of my sails. "Vinnie, listen to me," he said, shifting gears, fixing his gaze on me, steady, serious: "Listeners can love you and they can hate you. Either one is better than ambivalence. As long as they feel *something*."

Advertisers were. Feeling something, that is. They began lining up, and rates went right up with them. Glenn was already no slouch in the sponsorship dollar department, having some diehard believers (and fans) with businesses that would support him his entire run in New Haven, and the first few commercials that I was paid to do were absolutely Glenn spillover. They wanted Glenn but couldn't get him. So, they settled for the new guy.

But soon enough the first one requesting me turned up. It was a brand-new bar in town, and Glenn's newfound sobriety played as much a part of them going after me as me being "that guy" getting a lot of attention, plus someone born and raised in the very city where they were opening their bar.

The order came in for a :60 spot and the copywriter did her thing, rifling off come catchy copy, if not just a wee bit standard-issued. I was informed by the account executive whose client this bar was to pop over to the production studio after the show one morning and cut the spot. Glenn intervened.

"If it's okay," he said to her, "I'll just roll tape on the spot for Vinnie and shoot it over to production afterwards."

"That's so cute," this beautiful blond twenty-three-year-old selling machine cooed, to the point of teasing me. "He looks out for you!"

She was a very funny, very talented young lady who would later go on to do two things: One was tell me in confidence one day, "We're going to make a *lot* of money together." (We did.) The other was some ten years later going on to become a salesperson for

The Blaze during its infancy stages, Beck's website that ultimately became the foundation for his pay television network.

After the show I followed Glenn into another studio, where, armed with a printout of the commercial the station's copywriter churned out, I sat before a microphone. Glenn counted me down, *3-2-1*, and hit that record button like it was a snare drum.

I hit the ground running. No fumbles, no stumbles. No *breaths*. It sounded like I was saying these words about happy hour specials and juicy burgers while someone held a gun to my head. But I did it. In one take. At the end I looked over at Glenn, and after a beat he simply said, "Wow, that was *terrible*." We both burst out laughing while I managed to say "Whadda you want from me?" at the same time. Then he pressed stop and immediately began rewinding the now-archaic tape wrapped around its monster spool.

"For starters," he began while doing all this, "that was only forty-two seconds. *Slow down*."

That made sense. I felt like I was doing a 5K while I read the damn words. Okay, I'll go slower on the much-ballyhooed "take two."

But there wouldn't be one.

Glenn played it back for us both to hear, and what we'd just done came in at exactly sixty seconds, laughter, commentary and rebuttal included.

"I'd give them this," Beck said.

"Seriously?" I replied, although I both knew he was and, more importantly, understood why we should and agreed.

But we had to get by the AE (ad exec) and PD (program director) first. The former was smack dab on the exact same page as us, and the latter deemed it a bizarre suggestion and, worse, utterly unprofessional and potentially damaging to the station as a whole. There was a blooper left in! What's more, it's how the commercial ends!

The client loved it.

Others soon lined up wanting the same type of thing. The morning show soon sold out as far as advertisers were concerned, to the point of news and weather people managing to get cut pieces of the pie, as Glenn and I were beholden to certain sponsors who paid for each of us specifically to endorse them, thereby preventing us from taking on another client with a similar business.

But beyond that, the show soon became sold out in the "there is no more time for commercials" period. We began turning away business. Steering them to other dayparts.

It would remain that way for the entire three years.

My being immediately entranced by the world of radio did not mean that I did not remain steadfast in my continued determination to be a published author. I still wrote every day and pitched various publications, and *publishers*, on a regular basis. By this point, Beck and I were hitting movies constantly, wandering around the Barnes & Noble bookstore next door to the theater for long stretches either before or after what flick we'd be taking in. We were both huge movie fans.

I'd point out the types of books where I was hoping to first score, the little jokey and/or cutesy, self-helpy titles usually found in the "Stocking Stuffer" aisle. One joke/observation per page, tongue planted firmly in cheek, and yet somehow occasionally coming off as profound.

I showed Beck titles from some truly small houses—"boutique publishers," as they were known. They seemed the easiest nut to crack. I had my credits in some well-known publications, was now a radio host for what was then known as Clear Channel Radio, and seemed poised to at least land a little 100-pager. Then I'd be in. At least, that was my logic, and I was sticking to it.

Beck thumbed through one tiny little book, heavier on doodles than dialogue, and asked—rhetorically, one would presume—"Jesus, Vinnie, why even bother?" He jutted the book back in between copies of another, entirely different title, to add insult to injury, as if there were a contagion. He couldn't get it out of his hands quickly enough.

"That industry is in danger too," he'd declare on the drive home. By this point the eye rolls were beginning, but I hid them from him, except if we were on the air, facing each other, to goad him for comedic effect. I recall that night ending with me feeling as if he just felt like *everything* was in danger. I'd find out that he sure as hell did soon enough—and that this included not just the country, too, but mankind in general—yet the shot at publishing particularly stung. I'd give him radio; he'd inhabited that world long enough to know better than I. But I wouldn't give him publishing.

Glenn had his first book, *The Real America: Messages from the Heart and Heartland*, published in 2003. A mere three years into doing talk radio. Less, actually. He'd go on to have many books published, several of them going on to become *New York Times* bestsellers, including a novel! *The Christmas Sweater* was released in 2008, with Beck by this time also a TV star in his own right, with the controversial show bearing his name airing on Fox News.

While this development might appear to fly in the face of what he'd said to me that night at Barnes & Noble after we watched the latest Sylvester Stallone picture, it actually doesn't. Beck had shifted to message boards, essays on his page on the radio station website (where I still hadn't contributed a darn thing, or been asked to), and even podcasts long before most of those things even had those names. I want to say he'd begun writing himself during this period but it moreover came off as documenting. And it was good. Very good.

His demand that our rinky-dink operation in New Haven see to it that the web page for his show not only incorporate message boards (again, at this time, a largely foreign concept), but he wanted people to be able to "dial up" our show on their computers and watch us doing it. This would necessitate cameras, boom mics, modems, etc. Our engineers spiraled over his requests and coworkers (including myself) were lost as to why he wanted this and even what a lot of it even was, but Faith—who always had exactly that in her guy—agreed to every demand. (We were actually headed into a meeting with her to discuss the first billboard for his show that would include yours truly, and he turned to me and said, "Forget the billboard—just back me up when I ask for what I ask for." Recalling his cameo in my contract negotiation meeting, I did just that.)

He was ahead of the curve on the changes coming in radio and publishing, and even beyond, and as such mapped out how his brand could continue to be built and coexist with them. After his first few books performed quite well and confirmed his suspicions over just how much of a mess the publishing world was, he started his own imprint: Mercury Media Arts. His solution to all things entertainment would soon boil down to one rule of thumb: "Be your own boss."

His forward thinking would continue to serve as both blessing and curse.

In his 2010 bestseller *Broke: The Plan To Restore Our Trust, Truth, and Treasure* the opening paragraph to the Author's Note, which is wildly reminiscent, stylistically anyway, of the editorials he'd post on his page on the KC101 website, reads, "In the history of the world America's great experiment with freedom has been nothing more than a blink of the eye. Our way of life—unalienable rights, unquestionable freedom, unimaginable wealth—may seem natural and permanent to us, but, among the billions who have lived, we are the only ones to have ever experienced it. And now, I fear, we've never been so close to losing it."

Even so, in 1997 all was well. It was better than the previous year or two (or even three) had been, for both of us, personally *and* professionally. Beck was rejuvenated and would say as much. Often.

Each day's show was almost entirely improvised, which would eventually leave the guy with too much time on his hands, and become a bit of a problem. He had been accustomed to staying at the station the entire day, long after the show ended at ten a.m. There were conversations to be had, about what had worked and what hadn't on that day's show, and sketches to be written for the next day's, too. Now there was really no need for any of those things.

Sometimes we'd find ourselves in the middle of a funny, off-the-cuff bit and while a song played or commercial block aired, one of us would come up with an idea tied to where we'd just been. Like, "we should come back on the air to (insert celebrity here) calling in mad about what we just said" or "we should do a parody commercial about a product for what we were just talking about." The celebrity call-ins would be handled by moi, and we'd often go into those with our fingers totally crossed. I could do a lot of voices pretty good (Chris Farley, Rodney Dangerfield, Barbara Walters, Linus from "Peanuts," the mayor of New Haven and—the most popular of the lot—Glenn himself, to name but a few). Gallow's humor guy that Glenn is, my Farley didn't die with him (at the end of 1997); Beck loved going to the "Heaven Hotline," a bit he concocted where he'd call heaven and get whomever of the dearly departed we wanted and I'd run amok. (Yes, of course we called hell, too. Beck would tinker with something on the board that altered my voice for those, to get a demonic effect.)

The parody commercials, alternately, were written, and written quickly. If the song we were playing was three minutes and eighteen seconds that's exactly how long we had to prepare. Sometimes even to record it and have it ready for playback. That was rare, but we'd do it during those pre-Adobe Audition or Cool Edit days, when a huge reel sat behind the host of a show, and Glenn would wield an X-Acto knife like nobody's business and do the quickest, most precise edits imaginable. Sight to behold territory.

While he once told me he loved watching me write a parody commercial in record time, him always cast as narrator, and me usually performing two vastly different testimonials, he thrived on live. Even when written.

Glenn did voices, too. Adam West, of TV *Batman* fame, and Aunt Bea from the old, legendary *The Andy Griffith Show*. That's it. Finding places for these two became a galaxy quest, even if I could do pretty much everybody else who lived in Mayberry, from

Barney to Floyd the Barber to Gomer Pyle and even Goober. The joke became West and Bea popping up in the strangest of places.

We didn't write away from each other, at home, or even outside the hours of the morning show, although once an inspired Glenn beckoned me to his apartment where he spent the entire day writing a bit about searching in vain for Peeps for his daughters for Easter, as he'd waited too long and was discovering every store was sold out. It was to begin as a dutiful dad thinking he had the simplest of tasks before him, while his patience begins thinning and desperation tripling, only to finally find Peeps and emerge triumphant.

My assignment was to spend an hour or two listening to instrumentals on various CDs in that considerable collection of his to find the perfect accompaniment. The pace had to sync. It had to build as he was losing it. It had to crescendo upon his rallying cry that he'd found them. We found it on the soundtrack to the movie *City Slickers*. Maybe even *City Slickers 2*.

He performed it live at 6:35 on the Monday morning before Palm Sunday and nailed it (no pun intended). He didn't so much as stumble on a single word. Was it laugh-out-loud funny? To frazzled fathers and manic moms maybe. They weren't our target demo though, remember? Still, it was very entertaining, relatable, theatrical, and the stuff of blood, sweat, and tears. At 7:35 a.m. he did it again. And then again at 8:35. He nailed it every time. Upon listening to all three you probably couldn't even notice any glaring differences. He'd rehearsed it in front of me a dozen times the day before and clearly dozens more after I left his place.

Thing is, we had it on tape. He could have simply played back that first one, which he was happy with, the next two times. But he wanted to do it live every time out, potential blunders be damned. He heaved pressure upon himself. Challenged himself. He kept saying he could do it better, but he couldn't. He'd do it exactly the same, pitch-perfect, each time out. It was impressive, if not bordering on maniacal.

At one point during that show I revealed that the music was from the one copy of the *City Slickers* soundtrack ever purchased. Glenn asked what was wrong with buying movie soundtracks, and I replied that I'd purchased many, and one was even a favorite in my entire collection: Jon Bon Jovi's *Young Guns 2* soundtrack.

As was often the case, it was I now on the receiving end of the mockery. It was such a hot potato show, versus hot topic. I'd beat up on Glenn, then Glenn would beat up on me, then we'd both team up and give our bumbling news guy a hard time.

"Bon Jovi?" Glenn asked incredulously. The band itself—a favorite of mine since stumbling upon the making of the "Living On A Prayer" video in Los Angeles one summer day in 1986 and managing to be in the darn thing (go ahead and look)—was on a hiatus as the time, with Jon's next solo record, "Destination Anywhere," being readied for release any second. It was a great time to strike. They were inactive at the time, grunge was continuing to give many bands of their era a run for their money, and it was easy for him to deem the New Jersey rockers over and/or irrelevant. To even believe it.

I bypassed lauding "Blaze of Glory," a single that had won Bon Jovi a Golden Globe award and scored him an Oscar nomination, and went right for the extraordinary roster of talent Bon Jovi had managed to get to appear on the record: Jeff Beck, Little Richard, Elton John. Before Beck could dismiss that I asked, "Have you ever heard Jon Bon Jovi's version of Elton's 'Levon'? It's better than the original!"

Now I'd really done it. Beck found this equal parts blasphemous and preposterous, guffawing sardonically. He told me to bring my CD in the following day and we'd pit the versions against each other and have listeners call in to declare a winner. There were only what back then were referred to as "carts" as far as the music was concerned in the studio. No Internet to go to for an assist. There was a music library in the building, but it was a tiny little room and didn't even have Elton John's "Levon." The Elton that KC101 had was

"That's What Friends Are For" and songs from Disney movies I hadn't seen. In other words, I'd be bringing in Elton's "Levon," too.

The next day, both versions were played, with Bon Jovi's take being a decidedly '80s-fied one. It's a great version, and I love it, but I never said it was a superior version. I love the original. But Beck kept backing me into a corner, aghast that I could prefer the cover. I kept saying I didn't like one more than the other, but he kept saying I did. That's when I caught on. So, okay: Beck sided with Sir Elton and I sided with Sayreville's prodigal son.

For what Glenn wanted to take place over the next half or even full hour, we had to give listeners their "call to action" (radio speak). They had to choose, too: Beck's or mine; Elton's or Bon Jovi's. Surprisingly, Bon Jovi blew Elton out of the water. A madman across the water in fact. The calls went on and on and on, frantic women screaming Bon Jovi's name one after the other. Beck played that board like it was a piano. He was dumbfounded that Elton was losing by such a huge margin. So much so that I don't think he ever noticed that I was surprised myself. Just not to the extent that he was.

After the show the program director read us the riot act for an hour dedicated to playing one song that, at that time, was a quarter of a century old, and another that was never a single, and probably never even played on a radio station before. I sat there confused, as I was under the impression that Glenn Beck got to do whatever he wanted to do on *The Glenn Beck Morning Show*. He wanted the best for it. What's more, he knew what was best for it.

Our boss did not agree. At least, not with the Glenn knowing what was best for it part. Glenn let him be "Mister Middle Management" (a popular character on the show being born that day; Glenn would come to refer to the guy as this forevermore, eventually prompting me to start calling in *as him*, which involved me doing a nasally voice and talking like I was the coolest guy in the room, an "OG DJ," but utterly corny and nebbish; it was all very "Pig Vomit" from Howard Stern's "Private Parts"), and once he was done chastising, Beck simply leaned forward in his chair, stopping just short of hoisting himself out of it to tauntingly ask "That it?" It was.

The next day Jon Bon Jovi himself called in to the show live. He'd been apprised of the segment by our PD, and wanted to hear all about it, plus chat up his second solo record that would, again, be coming out soon. I viewed this as our boss extending an olive branch; Beck viewed it as a power play. Either way, I was live on the air with one of my favorite rockers since I was in high school, with Glenn saying before we went live with him for me to "take the lead and have fun." I'd interviewed plenty of musicians by this point, for print, with the focus being on them coming to town, but here I was the comedic sidekick on a morning radio show and the only singular goal being to entertain those listening. It was a trip.

A few months later Jon Bon Jovi would do a private solo concert for the radio station, with only contest winners in attendance. Again, Beck deferred to me, gifting me with the job of bringing Bon Jovi on stage, where he played the hits but also a few of his new solo songs. Glenn also gifted me with an autographed guitar from Bon Jovi, in honor of my turning thirty that summer. He'd bought the guitar for me, given it to me, and then shared that he'd be getting Jon to sign it at the concert. Which he did.

It was, by that point, the biggest radio event I was involved in yet, and it was simply exhilarating. The concert venue, of course, was the biggest club advertiser on the station at the time, the place where we held our weekly Saturday night dance party. How else to see to it that they extend that particular annual buy than by throwing them a bone every now and again? And this was a monster bone.

Every on-air personality was to be in attendance. We'd all be introduced one-by-one first, and then bring on the star of the night, a guy with a handful of big (and I mean big) hits on his resume, and then take turns interviewing him in between songs, even letting those contest winners get in on the act.

As the concert drew closer, it became obvious to me that no one's questions were going to be anything outside of your standard "what makes this new record different" and "do you have a favorite song" whereas I was fully prepared to dig deep, galvanize him with my intricate knowledge not only of his recording career, but of the music biz in general. And I did.

My first question, involving an early mentor of his, someone who'd never become a household name—outside of Jersey anyway (and probably only the Southside, wink, wink)—yet whose influence was touted by many a huge artist, caused his eyes to widen. My second, about an accolade he'd received early in his career, but that few knew about (a performance of his had inspired the series *Unplugged* on MTV) generated another arched eyebrow, a welcome reprieve from "how does it feel to be in such a small club when you've played huge arenas all over the world?" Yawn.

That's when my boss came over. The kudos were a'comin'! Maybe he'd even decided that I should handle the entire interviewing thing from this point on. "Your questions are too inside," he whispered to me. I giggled. Surely he was breaking my balls. "Nobody here, and definitely no one listening to this on the radio, knows what the hell you're talking about. Keep it simple."

Relieving me of my microphone, he whispered "watch" and flicked the button up: "Jon, are there any songs you get tired of performing live?"

CHAPTER FOUR

SEX & CANDY

One fall day, two women waltzed into the lobby, one of them very clearly having an air about her. She didn't necessarily look familiar, but she was hidden behind enormous sunglasses on a gray morning, it being barely eight o'clock obviously offending her, even while she managed a smile, decked out in designer leisurewear, looking around the lobby as if she had been there before.

She had. Some ten years earlier when she had a hit record.

But we didn't know that for a bit. Continuing on with our show, the two women disappeared into the studio next door, WELI—the news/talk station. A pop artist on a radio station that doesn't play music, next door to one that does. This couldn't have sat well with her, but such was the nature of the beast. Even I, ever the newbie, knew that. Those fifteen minutes of fame? Through radio I'd learn the last three or four more often than not suck. Even if you were a study in humility on the way up, that way back down, where only humble pie is served, is a relentless test of an artist's wherewithal and resolve.

They were in there for quite some time.

We continued the show, having long forgotten that these two women had been let into the building before Babs the receptionist had even punched in for the day, and we forged ahead with our banter, doing zany voices, taking random phone calls, and so forth. Then there they were again, in the lobby. The woman in the shades was listening to her counterpart speak a mile a minute, looking as if she was barely absorbing any of it, but staring at us doing our thing at the same time.

An intern spoke up at this point, alerting us to who this *was*, reminding us of the hit she had by humming a few bars, which almost got us there—and then she brought it home with that late '80s synth-fueled chorus. I smiled upon the recollection. My sister had loved that song. My girlfriend at the time had. A cover of it would surely be coming soon, probably on the soundtrack of a Michael Bay movie.

Next thing I knew there was a tap on the door. Glenn detested lightly tapping on the studio door. Better you gave a real knock. The only thing he detested more was someone simply bursting in. Especially with Babs not in yet. He told the intern to find out what they wanted. Wasn't it obvious? The whole situation was already awkward, en route to being awkwarder.

In less than a minute, the intern was peaking her head back into the studio and telling us that this talented singer who had managed a number one song in her lifetime was performing a free concert on the Green that night. *Did we want to talk to her about it?*

For the life of me I couldn't see why not. Yes, we were a Top 40 station, but the other dayparts did all sorts of "Blast From The Past" and "Flashback Friday" segments (long before the latter became a popular hashtag on then not-yet-invented social media sites), plus Glenn did as he pleased anyway. Besides, it had been a *huge* hit. A number one song is no easy feat, which not a lot of people realize, and evidently many of those people work(ed) in the very business that was supposed to convey it was.

This was pre-*Dancing With The Stars* and all of the other reality TV shows that remind us of the once-exalted, revisit, catch up, and humiliate. Glenn scoffed at the notion.

Our mortified intern need not pass this on, as it was clearly heard through the cracked studio door. The singer's handle—who could have easily been someone working for the town chamber of commerce hosting this show on the Green or working for a record label or just a personal assistant—shouted over the intern's head, "She's got a new record coming out," in an effort to suggest relevance.

I got a glimpse of the singer's face. The star quality lingered, her cheekbones high, rosy, lips full. Just because you're not a star anymore doesn't mean star quality disappears. She had it. In spades. She seemed nonplussed by the whole thing, while Glenn mouthed to the intern "No."

They both just left after that. She didn't burst in and give him a piece of her mind, or break down in tears, or even toss him a nice *fuck you*. They just . . . left.

The exits in the entertainment industry go from frenzied, security-laden affairs, where sometimes disguises are necessary, to right on out the very door you came in, maybe someone there to ask for an autograph, maybe not.

"What if this new song of hers winds up being a hit?" I asked of Beck.

"You know what *what if* is?" he countered.

"An underappreciated Marvel comic?" I offered.

Unflinching, yet wearing a quizzical expression thanks to my semi-facetious answer, he told me, in no uncertain terms: "Morning show cancer."

Fall was billboard season. Discussions began on Beck's latest one being the first with someone else's name on it since Pat Gray's exit years earlier. Mine.

Faith wanted to do something straight out of the morning radio playbook. Something gimmicky. Beck was vocal about the idea she'd resurrected having been done to death, and you could plainly see that this was a man with a terminal case of "been there, done that," in dire need of catharsis, even if he did ultimately concede that it would be effective.

It was to go like this:

The billboard would read THE GLENN BECK MORNING SHOW **6-10AM**. That would all be in a bright yellow, which would be the same bright yellow KC101 boasted. Interestingly, the KC101 now appeared stretched across an enormous globe—Earth, if you will—with the tippity-top protruding outside the perimeters of said billboard. It was eye-popping. This brand new logo for the decades-old Top 40 station had been designed by Beck himself. His creativity was in complete alignment with his desire to gut all things, freshen everything up, if not abandon it all together.

I was instructed to immediately take issue on the air with the fact that my name was nowhere to be found on the billboard. Faith wanted me to fire listeners up and spur them into action. That action would take the form of listeners calling in to show their solidarity, and agree—nay, demand!—that this most grievous of errors be rectified. In fact, I was to get to that point myself. Mine was to be a slow boil. Disbelief at first, but then a slow and steady journey to outrage. Make it last two weeks. By the end of the second week, the reveal: WITH VINNIE PENN would appear beneath the **6-10AM**, looking like it was spray painted on by a hooligan. Like the people have spoken!

I voiced a particular concern. I didn't think I could do it. Not well anyway. I feared I wouldn't be convincing, plus this was also in stark contrast to who I was at the time and, more importantly, who those tuning in had been getting to know and, for the most part, liking: a guy who didn't care about a damn thing. Me caring about my name appearing on the morning show's new billboard would be inauthentic, never mind the faux outrage I was to conjure up, and the bratty asking of listeners if they agreed that I should be on there.

Faith had exactly that again though. In spades. In Beck. In me. She had that shit to spare. She just smiled that enormous smile of hers, hands clasped, saying over and over, "You'll do great."

On our way out of the office, Glenn told me not to worry about it, and that it was an old bit that always worked. He never spoke down to his audience, but he knew there was a certain degree of "give away tickets to caller 101" and 101 people call for them going for the whole thing. If you ask them, they will call.

On the morning after the billboard went up I didn't say a word. I couldn't get there. Glenn began prodding me.

"Have you seen the new billboard, Vinnie?"

"How d'ya like it?"

"Do you feel like it's missing anything?"

He was shooting me antagonistic looks, and I was cupping my microphone, snickering. It just wasn't going to happen.

After that show Faith—and even Mr. Middle Management—ripped into me. Into us. We were on a timeline here. We'd wasted an entire day. We had nine now until my name would appear in a graffiti font, with five of the letters appearing as if the paint were dripping.

On day two, Glenn simply took the reigns. He began saying that I should be hacked off that my name wasn't on there, that it was a slap in the face, and that I'd earned it. He asked if listeners agreed. The phone lines lit up. The rest of the week played out this way, the following one kicking off with Glenn now saying he was angry. He was angry *for* me. I deserved this. He asked if listeners were with him. The phones lit up again.

That Friday he staged a walkout. I watched in awe as the entire charade played out, revealed even more of this world that was radio.

Glenn declared he'd had enough, that this wrong being done unto me was too much to bear, and that the two of us would be leaving mid-show to go to the diner down the street until management caved to his demand. Righted this wrong. Listeners were welcome to join us.

The line to get in went down the street.

Faith did not like this change in execution one single bit. Our program director liked it even less. It was like Glenn got final cut on *their* film. But heaven forbid they share this with him. I got all of it, and it would mark the beginning of impromptu meetings held with me, where Glenn was nowhere in sight. I often left wondering if I should run back to him and fill him in. Sometimes I did, and sometimes I didn't.

For Faith it was just a matter of her wanting it executed the way it had been discussed. She also *hated* the walkout. But it's not like she shared this discontent without that huge smile on her face.

(Incidentally, I believe the walkout was Glenn's favorite part. It was the direction he decided to take after that first day of me failing to do my part. He wanted to see just how invested fans really were in the show. How far they were willing to go. It had less to do with me than it did Glenn seeing if the show's listeners were all in with him. He needed that at that time, and this tired promotion inadvertently lent him the vehicle. Without such, he'd have never been able to do what he did so convincingly. Or comfortably.)

For Mr. Middle Management it was far more insidious. He mocked me. He told me Glenn had hijacked the whole darn thing, made it all about him, and came away looking like a hero. He couldn't believe I "let him play me like that" and basically looked down at me the entire time, punctuating each thought with a hearty, condescending laugh. It was very 1970s middle school playground.

I didn't take the bait. In the end, Glenn simply wanted the reveal of the new billboard over with, and I couldn't pull the trigger. He had groaned at the point in the meeting when we were told to drag it out for two weeks in the first place. That was an awful lot of time, and he had much more that he wanted to do. He was finally excited about his show again, about radio again, about his career again, and had many avenues he wanted to explore.

It all boiled down to one word: Storyline. Glenn believed the show needed one, that it was a key ingredient to any successful morning radio show, and every time he mentioned that word to our program director the guy would be flummoxed. He had no idea what Glenn meant by storyline and would get visibly agitated. Glenn wanted Tuesday's show to pick up where Monday's left off, which would pick up where our Friday cliffhanger left off, and so on. He wanted not just recurring characters, but their returns largely being about where we'd last left them.

Glenn wanted the radio show to mirror a television sitcom. In fact, he did so much that he had me write a theme song for the show and we got it recorded by Christine Ohlman, "The Beehive Queen" herself, the long-running vocalist for the Saturday Night Live Band, who not only lived nearby, but I had exacted a relationship with the guy running the studio where she recorded much of her solo work.

We had already begun delving into the local music scene—an absolute no-no for the Top 40 station in *any* town (unbeknownst to me, of course)—and whenever we'd have a local band in to perform or play a song of theirs off a CD, Mr. Middle Management would come in with bloody knuckles. The dashboard of his car took such a beating for the short time he oversaw Glenn's show with me as his sidekick.

But, Ohlman was, at the very least, a little bit different than, say, the ska/hard rock outfit whose lead singer performed shirtless and had painted the entire upper half of his body (including his face), to promote a gig at a pool joint that night that—gasp!—*wasn't even an advertiser on the show*. Ohlman was part of the SNL Band, having become lead vocalist for them the same year Glenn arrived in New Haven: 1991. She done back-up vocals on a Stones record. Yes, The Rolling Stones!

The title of the theme song for "The Glenn Beck Morning Show with Vinnie Penn" was "They Have No Talent." It was all about how neither of us had any. How we weren't funny, entertaining, even smart in any way, shape, or form. After I presented the lyrics to Glenn and he signed off on them with a chuckle, he grabbed a notepad and covered it with chicken scratch for me to give to Ohlman. (Less chicken scratch than it was in a sort of indecipherable code—to me anyway—as Beck's penmanship was a thing of beauty.)

I attended the recording session at Trod Nossel Studios in neighboring Wallingford, a storied recording studio, where blues legend Pinetop Perkins recorded and mixed "Born in the Delta" that very year—1997—and emerged with a Grammy nomination. Fleetwood Mac had recorded there. The owner, Thomas "Doc" Cavalier, was a former dentist whose dream of running a recording studio became reality there, and with it a very close relationship with Andrew Loog Oldham, manager and producer of the Stones. Also, a very, *very* close relationship with Ohlman herself.

But I didn't just attend—I played harmonica on the track. If memory serves, we did no more than three or four takes, and then I handed both "Doc," who was producing the track, and Christine, Glenn's scribble. He was requesting they isolate the bass line and give him one strum of that separately, plus also just the final rousing chorus of "They Have No Talent" separately. I had no idea why.

Shortly thereafter, he'd begun using each of those short musical interludes as outros. If we scored a laugh with each other (or at the other's expense is more like it), or with a guest or listener, he'd cue up one as a buffer of sorts, to take us into commercial breaks. I mean, why bother saying "We'll be right back" when you can convey it with a quirky little music outro.

The isolated bass line was the one that really struck me. It not only was in keeping with the actual theme song, obviously, but it was reminiscent of the bass line for *Seinfeld*, which was at its cultural zenith at the time, used in the exact same way on the series.

Beck's unwavering belief that any morning radio show worth listening to have a storyline got its final flourish from us incorporating this self-deprecating, "throwbacky" theme song into the show. The irony was lost on neither of us that we were inspired by the infamous "show about nothing" to do something to further establish that ours was a show about something.

But Beck's affinity for *Seinfeld* would not end there.

In the fall of 1997 Glenn managed to sell an advertiser on the idea of a "Seinfeld Watch Party" every Thursday night. That's right: You, Mr. Bar Owner, pay both Glenn and his sidekick their going rates for personal appearances, and we'll be here every Thursday from eight to ten, but at nine o'clock sharp we'll watch the latest episode of *Seinfeld* on the enormous TV you have set up for football with everyone in the bar. Pay us to watch TV with your crowd.

Shockingly, the guy went for it.

Shockingly, the place was packed every time.

Tragically, Jerry Seinfeld would declare this the final season of his show.

After shaking off the shackles of my disbelief that Glenn got someone to bankroll this weekly raiding of their register, I showed up for the first one and saw that our promotions team had diligently set up chairs across the mingling area, and sometime dance floor. It looked like a ramshackle theater. Row upon row of seats. I didn't envision people sitting down when it came time to watch a given episode. I didn't even envision them watching it.

But, sit they did, and watch they did.

Glenn devised it so that we'd spend the first forty-five minutes or so that we were there playing *Seinfeld* trivia with the crowd, wherein if they knew it was "no soup for you" or "the sea was angry that day, my friend," they'd score a KC101 T-shirt. Then we'd hop on mic one last time right before the episode began to ask everyone to take their seats and prepare to watch. You could hear a pin drop for the next twenty-two minutes.

After a few times of doing this, the crowd—predominantly, if not entirely, female—began wanting to watch *Friends*, too. We essentially were asked if we could get paid to watch more TV. We loved *Friends*, so that was just fine by us. It quartered our contest time, but no one seemed to mind. If anything, we just moved faster when it came to that and still unloaded every T-shirt, ice scraper, and koozie.

We were both still single, and one of us was enjoying the hell out of it, while the other was growing tired of it.

At one of our *Seinfeld* nights, we both left with a date on our arm to catch what was left of a Sheryl Crow concert taking place maybe ten minutes from where we were. The women were both coworkers, but they were coworkers we were definitely interested in. We enjoyed the concert together but then paired off and went our separate ways.

The next morning, I was damaged goods. I was hungover, and my date (someone I actually knew even before I began working at the station, where she was a top-notch salesperson) and I had gone back to her place to devour each other. One of the interns noted my disheveled appearance, but it wasn't the first time they'd seen me show up in this condition. It was the first time, however, that I'd inform them that the whole darn thing had begun as a double date with Beck. We couldn't wait to see how he'd turn up!

It was a close call. Glenn was never late for the show, but he was never early, either. The perks of your morning radio job being right around the corner. This was his closest to being late ever. My, what a story he'd have to tell! Could it top mine!?

We spotted his car whiz into the parking lot with less than two minutes to spare. He flew into the building, and subsequently the studio, with great zeal, and in lieu of cuing up the show's theme song, opted instead for the Ace of Base hit "Beautiful Life," and gave it one whopper of an introduction.

While the song played, we caught up. I said little more than it was a great night that got more than a little crazy and expressed some concern that it was with a coworker. While I adored her, and had since we first met as teenagers, I didn't see us getting serious after this, and the conversation that would take place after the show was definitely going to be a tricky one. Glenn, however, had no such concerns. He was interested in seeing where things could go with this new woman in his life and his great night, too, had gotten more than a little crazy: "They painted until the sun came up." No typo. They stood side-by-side, both with an easel before them, and painted. For *hours*.

As was the case with the show we were doing, the majority of that day's installment was born during that exchange. We'd go on to share with the audience what had happened the night before—leaving out that it was with coworkers—and each taking swipes at the other for how their night ended. Where Glenn would call me an animal, I'd call him Bob Ross. I was gross, he a geek. Soon enough, he was asking listeners to call in with which way they'd want their night to go, and call in they did. I am aware that this type of radio continues to this day but considerably less, and *all* of it is pretaped, with many of the callers staged, if not straight up trained performers. Yes, even the callers.

These were the waning glory days of *anything goes* radio, and the listeners more often than not matched us every step of the way in outrageousness. Glenn's night got its votes (and gushing), and mine got its (and lusting). Glenn broke everything down to listeners choosing, and much of the time I'd never see it coming. I've no recollection who "won," by the way. I think Glenn?

The conversation awaiting me after the show did not go as expected. She was very sweet, but nervous herself, and for an entirely different reason. She had a crush on someone else at work and swore me to secrecy that he'd never find out what happened. She had high hopes they'd some day get together. I promised my lips were sealed, and made sure Beck didn't say anything about it either.

Beck's romance proved short-lived. A few months, tops. But, they were happy ones, full of Broadway shows and museum visits, before he ultimately called things off, needing his love life to fire on every cylinder just like he needed his radio show to.

He needn't worry, though. In just a few months time, he'd meet another woman, at one of our "Seinfeld Watch Parties," who'd change his life.

I'd meet one who'd do the same for me. A beautiful college student nine years younger than me; we'd proceed to date for several years. Twenty years later she'd be famous, starring in the smash reality series *The Real Housewives of Beverly Hills*. Dorit Kemsley would become a household name, but back then she was Dorit Lemel, a vivacious, intoxicating bon vivant sketching designs in a notebook while waiting for me at local watering holes, daydreaming that those designs would one day become an actual fashion line. They did.

CHAPTER FIVE

BULLET WITH BUTTERFLY WINGS

Just a few months before all of this, though, tragedy struck in the Elm City. A twenty-one-year-old unarmed black man was shot and killed in New Haven by a white police officer from neighboring East Haven. The story was ugly all the way around. It was April 1997, and it had all begun as a routine traffic stop. But he led the officer on a chase that crossed town lines. The chase ended in a vacant lot, where the officer exited his vehicle, weapon aimed at the windshield of the car he'd just chased down. The driver opted to hit the gas and careen toward him. He was shot several times at close range and died at the scene.

I genuinely do not recall if I was taken aback when Glenn brought this up on the show the following morning. It was in stark contrast to how we typically began our show, loose and silly and exchanging good mornings. Glenn came outta the gate being quite descriptive about the "bloodbath," jarring for people bathing their cereal with milk at 6:06 a.m.

I always simply followed Glenn's lead. And, again, for all I knew this was what any Top 40 morning radio host would do, despite the rumblings having already begun that Glenn covered some stories management would prefer he didn't and—in those days anyway—most Top 40 hosts probably would most definitely *not*. Still, I followed.

What I brought to the table: I was the New Haven lifer. I was born and raised in the very city where this took place and knew the area well. I also knew East Haven well, having graduated from East Haven High School in 1985. I could speak to the side streets and off-ramps, the dead ends and the ditches, the reputation and the devastation.

What Glenn brought to the table: Back the blue. Long before it was ever even a slogan.

Glenn backed the officer straightaway. And while I said I do not recall if I was taken aback when he brought the story up, I was sure as hell taken aback by him staying on it the entire show, and the next day's show, and the following few *weeks*.

When the number of shots fired came in, I expressed disbelief at just how many there were. They all hit their mark. Why keep shooting? These were some of my preliminary observations. I also knew that the East Haven PD was incessantly dogged with allegations of racism and misogyny. I didn't know if any of that was true, but the local paper sure led with that often, and continues to over two decades later. That being in the back of my mind probably colored my initial stance on the whole thing.

To be clear, I back the blue too. I don't even know how these people do what they do on a daily basis. A childhood friend became one and watching him kiss his small children goodbye, then making a crack to me that he hoped that wasn't the last time he'd ever see them, really struck a chord with me. That is the gig, though, isn't it? *Bye. Love you. Hope I don't get killed in the line of duty today.*

They run *toward* gunfire, Molotov cocktails, pipe bombs and bloodcurdling screams. They run toward what people are running *from*. How do you not back that?

That said, Glenn described what went down and my real-time response was what it was. Weren't two bullets to the chest enough?

He'd emptied the gun. Despite it being some twenty-five years before George Floyd, I just knew where this could go, even if my gut told me this cop had probably never discharged his weapon before except for training practice, was nervous as hell, adrenaline colliding with that anxiousness, his innermost hope being getting to that sweet pension without ever taking a life. (For the record, I was wrong there: This same officer had actually already shot at another unarmed twenty-one-year-old black man, some six years earlier, but missed.)

Glenn bared his fangs, condemning the media coverage of the story and the actions of the deceased. He'd led the officer on a high-speed chase. He'd gunned the car and driven straight toward him. Vehicular manslaughter anyone? Most important of all, Glenn noted that those first two shots did *not* stop the driver. The car did not veer. In fact, he gave it more gas.

The following day Glenn picked up right where he left off. The entire show was about it. There'd been someone else in the car with the deceased. He'd done some talking in the twenty-four hours that had passed. Both he and the driver were high on PCP and other drugs. I felt as if someone shot in the chest high on PCP would slump over at the wheel instantly; Glenn delivered an impassioned diatribe about how PCP tricks the brain into thinking you're a superhero and that, unbeknownst to the driver, he was dying, despite feeling as if he had the strength of ten men. It was a powerful, if not speculative, rant.

By the end of the show the officer's wife was waiting for him in the lobby, teary-eyed, confiding what an unbelievable toll this was taking on her husband. Soon enough squad cars filled the parking lot of the radio station. Glenn's solidarity met with a visceral affection by a handful of cops, and my questions and thoughts deemed valid, understandable, and, most important of all, key to keeping an intricate dialogue going. (Interestingly, thinking back, I do recall at one point stressing how much I supported the police to Glenn during a commercial break, but that I struggled with reconciling with the emptying an entire weapon into his chest. Glenn applauded my being forthright with such potentially unwelcome questions, with being true to myself, which he prided himself on, and encouraged me to continue challenging not so much him, but the story that the local press was feeding us.)

For the remainder of our time doing the show together, police would turn up at all of our charity events, offer thanks and assistance, feeling indebted to Beck and inviting me out for drinks with them when their shifts ended.

Covering that story went on for months, and even as it slowly tapered off, it truly remains the only time in the three years that we worked together that I felt like Glenn Beck was breaking every single rule in the Top 40 Radio Rulebook. And I'll cop—pun intended—to two things: One, it made me nervous. But two, I dug it. That the show was this mish-mosh of slapstick and serious, of pranks and pontificating, of quips and quest.

That case remains the highest-profile officer-involved shooting in New Haven and among the most notorious officer-involved shootings in Connecticut history. The officer stayed on until retirement, and as of this writing the corner where the shooting took place had just gotten approval to be renamed after the victim's mother.

One day, as our coverage of it ramped up, management nudged Beck, reminding him that "we've got a news station ya know. It's the studio right next door to yours." Our PD theatrically pointed it out and Glenn took a good, long look at it, saying nothing. Not long after, that studio got a complete renovation, while the ol' fifty-watt blowtorch was snubbed. WELI was now state-of-the-art and KC101 was a relic, with a temperamental board that Beck would occasionally have to pop open and take a wire cutter and electrical tape to, a mechanic and his jalopy, an artist and his palette. Little did they know, one day in the not-too-distant future, Glenn would soon be moving in next door. Albeit briefly.

As summer came to a close, I crossed state lines for the three-day weekend, spending Labor Day in the Ocean State. I had my shoe size 11 cell phone with me, same number to this day, one of the first off the assembly line. Beck hadn't even gotten one himself yet. It was the days before texting and sexting and posting and roasting and GPS and TMI. You really just used it to *call* people who you knew were away.

It was August 31, and my phone rang at an early enough hour to wake my bedmate and prompt her to ask at least three probing questions before I could figure out where I was: who I was, where my phone was, and who it was on it. It was Glenn. Diana, Princess of Wales, had died.

Hers was a life cut as tragically short as it was mysteriously and prophetically. It was a harbinger of things to come, the paparazzi turning it up more than a few notches for those shots that'd get them tens of thousands of dollars, risk of injury be damned. (Britney would soon be taking a bat to their windshields and Alec Baldwin knocking them out with one punch.)

We'd already touched upon the States' fascination with all things Diana many times, both Beck and I on the same page as far as being puzzled at the fandom. Women would call in to the show to tell us they remembered the day they watched her marry Prince Charles on television, them and their mother, the American Girl's 1981 Super Bowl. We'd ask them why they cared so much, what the menu included on that day, if there were hors d'oeuvres. Standard morning radio stuff.

We did the same with the divorce. That came in 1996, after phone conversations between Charles and now-Queen Camilla were released to the public (amidst myriad other public humiliations for the late princess). As such, it was even still fertile ground when our show began, with Charles managing to go from hot water to scalding, while late-night hosts continued to mock what he deemed "sweet talking" and SNL dedicated entire sketches to it. I'd call in as Charles and Glenn would ask me if I really wanted to be a tampon. Not necessarily groundbreaking as far as morning radio was concerned, but my Charles was solid, and Glenn would encourage me to test the boundaries of what I thought was the FCC's wrath but instead was the PD's. I'd use words I was not sure were deemed usable, gauging Beck's reaction to know when to reign it in. (I recall one stern talking to from my PD behind Glenn's back where the guy told me not to use words like boner or hard-on, but to instead go with the technical term, [i.e., erection]. "But a Brit saying boner is funnier!" I exclaimed.)

But the death, and the horrific manner in which it occurred, spawned coverage on our show that spiraled quickly. It began with Glenn delivering a touching, even uplifting, eulogy. Then we began taking calls from brokenhearted women, extolling the virtues of her grace and beauty, her one-of-a-kindness and charitable nature—none of whom could do so without a reference to the highly rated Royal Wedding and Mom's Catering.

From there Glenn began what would become a monthlong tear on the paparazzi and, more importantly, the mainstream media took its next beating. This was beyond invasion of privacy, bordering on take-no-prisoners territory. Further, Glenn vented, the media footing the bill for it was repugnant, as it could—and would—pave the way for more deadly chases. He saw culpability and lamented the fact that there didn't seem to be a single publisher who would not only turn down what was basically a photo shoot but make a very public statement that he or she would be and why. "The media is the real enemy here," he said at one point.

This was 1997!

The real rub became, wasn't that us?

That's the way our PD saw it. Beck was calling for the chopping down of a tree we were very much a branch on. In our own admittedly small way.

But "Mr. Middle Management" conveying this concern didn't come straightaway. And that takedown, too, would be delivered before an audience of one: Me.

Next up in Glenn's coverage regarding the death of Diana was the possibility that death might not be the right word for him, or us, to be using. *Was murder more fitting?*

He began deep-dives on Dodi Fayed, who—along with his Egyptian businessman father—rubbed Beck the wrong way. What did he stand to gain? Could he have been a puppet master here? Could he have been in cahoots with Charles?

And what of Charles? Could he have masterminded this "accident"? He tried in vain to get Paul Burrell, Diana's butler and confidant, on the show. He'd published a note in 1993, while Glenn was still doing the KC101 show with Pat, that he claimed Diana had written about having a very real fear that this was in the works.

Next up: Britain's MI6. Glenn saw their hands as more than dirty—they were straight up bloody. There were murmurings from across the pond that MI6 was monitoring Diana before her death. Why? Beck was doling out conspiracy theories before we called them that. Of note: A former MI6 officer claimed in a sworn statement to the French inquiry some two years later that Britain's MI6 was involved in the crash, and this came after he went on record saying that he believed one of her bodyguards was a contact for British Intelligence.

As quickly as the theories could be debunked, Beck was ready with another. What's more, our listeners smelled a rat, too—but just one: Charles. That said, they never expounded after saying so, instead opting to comment on how handsome William was and what a fairytale possibly lay in wait for an American. They'd "fix him up on-air." Despite only being fifteen, names like Jennifer Love-Hewitt, Alicia Silverstone, and Reese Witherspoon were bandied about.

Mr. Middle Management enjoyed that morning's segment, the first to his liking in two full weeks. He was a master of passive aggression, but up against someone with zero respect for him. Beck paid him absolutely no mind. "Do more segments like that," he said to Glenn one morning, a heretofore unheard compliment, as he entered the studio to say it. Entering the studio, too, was a rarity. He never came into the studio while we were doing the show, which I didn't realize was something earmarked as the sign of a bad program director. As Glenn one day told me: "There's nothing a PD should ever have to say that he can't say at 10 a.m." Beck nodded along, but Mr. Middle Management couldn't leave well enough alone, quickly adding, "if you *have to* keep talking about it." Glenn played it cool, but turned beet red when the guy left, and was absolutely livid. I expected them to finally have it out, and the over/under was week's end.

But Elton John came to the rescue.

By mid-September Reg returned to the studio—and a classic—all to honor his fallen friend. The classic was "Candle in The Wind," his heartbreaking, chart-topping ode to Norma Jean (aka Marilyn Monroe). He saw parallels between the two icons, if not iconoclasts. Produced by George Martin (aka "The Fifth Beatle"), lyrics were tweaked by legendary counterpart Bernie Taupin to be about Diana, and the global proceeds would go to her many charities.

"Candle in The Wind 1997" entered the UK singles chart at number one after only one day of sales, giving John his fourth UK number one single, and it went on to become the bestselling single in UK chart history. But stateside it took a little bit longer. Still, in October it became Sir Elton's ninth US number one hit single and topped the much-ballyhooed *Billboard* Hot 100 for fourteen weeks, going on to be the bestselling single in *Billboard* history. John even won a Grammy for it, at the 40th Annual Grammy Awards in 1998.

Accolades aside, Glenn and I immediately took to deigning it—well, not so much a cash grab as a relevancy grab—for Reg. Both huge fans of the rock legend and inarguably gifted pianist, the dust from the "Levon" debacle had barely settled and we found ourselves mocking the new lyrics and wondering if this was going to be the new phase of his career: Constantly reworking "Candle" to be about the latest dead celebrity. Gallows humor, to be sure, and irreverent as hell, but this was where we landed, and we had a lot of laughs with our audience while we were there.

Added bonus? Mr. Middle Management actually found this morbid digression considerably more palatable for our listeners than Glenn delivering impassioned speeches about the shortness of life or spinning intricate conspiracy theory webs and bashing the mainstream media.

We immediately took to recording our own versions of "Candle," the first dedicated to none other than legendary actor Jimmy Stewart, who died just a month before Diana, and had been spending many of his final days doing late-night TV appearances where he read poetry he'd written about his dog. The lyrics wrote themselves thanks to that, and I sang it *as* Stewart, while Glenn managed to find the "Candle in The Wind" music bed in our production studio. He jutted the cart into place, delivered a galvanizing introduction, and cued up the music. I sang it live on the air. But for this, and the few that would follow, we'd roll tape and play it back.

Next up came "Candle in The Wind October 1997" (the Stewart one had no title when introduced but later became known as "Candle in The Wind Retroactive"). This second one was dedicated to folk icon and '70s *Oh God* movie star John Denver, who died tragically in a curious airplane mishap. I sang that one doing my best Elton.

After that there was easily the biggest hit of them all, "Candle in The Wind Down by the River," dedicated to funnyman Chris Farley, whose death, albeit tragic, was not altogether surprising and easily lent itself to celebrating his life. I sang that one as Farley's popular *SNL* character, motivational speaker Matt Foley. Listeners began requesting it, even outside of our show. Mr. Middle Management, we would later find out, gave strict orders that it not be played outside of "The Glenn Beck Show with Vinnie Penn."

He and Glenn had had a near miss as far as finally having it out once and for all, thanks to Elton John's tribute to his beloved friend and us running with it in, well, a very *SNL* way. Or so we liked to think.

Parody had proven salve.

CHAPTER SIX

A LONG DECEMBER

When the ambulance roared up to the front of the building, sans sirens blare, everyone exchanged curious glances as if we just might be in the middle of some big prank. This was still the age of guerrilla radio, long before your Internet and satellite and Spotify and hustling, bustling thumbs on devices Stephen Hawkings himself couldn't see coming; competing radio stations regularly tried to fuck with you.

Was the classic rock station only blocks away—the station playing music from bands that meant everything to me, like Van Halen, Queen, and Motley Crue, while I played a hit-and-miss game heavy on the miss with the Top 40 songs in the country according to *Billboard* magazine on a daily basis—alerting 9-1-1 to a "danger" one of us was in, scant months before *69 would change the game?

After all, it was common practice during the days of guerrilla radio for one station to send a hearse to their competitor, music format notwithstanding, essentially sending the message: "We've killed you. You're dead. This is for your funeral. You're welcome. Rest in peace."

We quickly dismissed such a notion, as our main competition was a morning radio team who had been together fifteen years and, quite frankly, were certain New York or Los Angeles awaited. Despite the fact that it had been *fifteen years already*. They were cocksure, had the sizable crowds at their events to back the attitude up, and would surely view such a move as possibly being perceived as them breaking a sweat over us. They couldn't have that. Better to behave as if they didn't know if the show were still on the air.

So, was the ambulance for the news/talk station down the hall? Things occasionally got hairy in there. The liberal co-host and the conservative co-host of the midday "Crossfire" (or something like that) show kept taking swings at each other. Death threats came in rapid fire, as regularly as we got requests for pop songs. The KKK even rolled in one day, as if they wouldn't stand out at all. They did. (Note: That is an absolutely *chilling* thing to see in real life.)

Then it dawned on us that a popular singer/songwriter was scheduled for a pretaped performance late morning. Maybe news of it leaked . . .? Management being proactive? He was on his fifth or sixth straight Top Ten hit at the time, so the thought of some frazzled young ladies out in the parking lot, waiting for him to show, hearts racing like they're at the airport amid Beatlemania, and then one drops from the excitement didn't seem far-fetched. Then we thought better of that, too. I mean, ambulances don't work that way.

By then the EMTs came racing *in* the building, so parking lot girl fainting was definitely ruled out. For a moment I thought that it was the singer himself, a well-known partier, quasi-fresh from a stint in rehab, having issues of his own and his manager having called ahead to the radio station. *Meet us at the station* and all that. Heck, maybe he punched a wall in a fit of temperamental artist rage and now needed stitches. And it was the hand he strummed with. SO rock 'n roll.

That reverie was demolished upon the sight of four—count 'em *four*—EMT workers carrying someone out on a stretcher in record time. We stepped out into the lobby, lost amid the chaos, separated in a flash like kids from their parents at an amusement park.

When we reconvened in the studio we spoke in hushed tones. It was an account executive. A salesman. He had dropped to the floor mid-pitch, on the telephone, sweating profusely and heart racing. *Very Glengarry Glenn Ross*. The pressure bested him. He was *this close* to closing a deal that would, in the end, have generated maybe six grand for the station, $250 of it for him.

He never came back to work, but I saw him some years later, DJing a carnival.

Midway through our first year together Beck seemed to have only two things on his mind: Getting our show syndicated (he'd not yet met the woman who'd change—or, as he so often likes to put it, save—his life) and "Stuff-A-Bus," an annual fundraiser he'd created upon settling in Connecticut. This yearly food drive had become Beck's calling card during his time at KC101, even more so after partner Pat's departure, and still takes place to this day, well over a quarter of a century after him parting ways with the station. That's a testament to too many things to list here.

One of these two things would cause the first rift in our relationship, and it obviously wasn't his sudden obsession with getting "The Glenn Beck Morning Show with Vinnie Penn" syndicated. Glenn became laser focused on that due to his certainty that local radio, as he knew and loved it, was doomed. The exit sign could be seen from our studio. The expiration date was flying at us. I thought it all a bit theatrical but, again, this world was so new to me I figured anything was possible. All the same I'd tune him out when it came to that. I was just too happy.

Would I mind if Beck scored us a syndication deal? Obviously not. Even if in the back of my mind I knew half the reason I was going over so well was because I was a townie. I was born and raised in the city where we were on the air. I knew all the ins and outs, nooks and crannies, and so on. Plus, would a Vinnie fly in Indiana? I wasn't so sure. But it's not like I objected. Even if—beyond these slight concerns—I was just fine doing what we were doing, day in and day out, for the *rest* of my days. This was all more than enough for me.

But not Beck. I'd soon learn nothing was ever enough for Beck. Such are the markings of either madmen or millionaires. The former is what I thought left KC101 just a few years later, but the latter is what he'd become, and in a fairly short matter of time, too.

One morning Glenn came in and caught me having some laughs with the overnight guy. "Dan Marino" did the midnight–6:00 a.m. shift. His nom de plume was the brainchild of Mr. Middle Management, who had two of the on-air staff change their names from what he felt were overly ethnic, difficult to pronounce ones, to—for whatever reason—popular footballers at the time. Now, the overnight guy was one thing. But he had a popular college kid doing nights shed his Italian last name in favor of "Kerry Collins." He just one day began referring to himself as that instead of saying his God-given name. I honestly thought some listeners would call in asking if he was okay, or maybe dial up 911, thinking this some sort of breakdown playing out in real time. But the imaging for his show had been changed to reflect the change too, and he's been Kerry Collins ever since. He's still with the station to this day!

After "Dan" left the studio Glenn warned me not to get too close to him. I assumed this meant he was about to share something deep and dark about the dude. But it was simply that "overnight guys will be completely gone from radio in a year's time."

Yeesh. "More of this talk," I thought to myself. Our overnight guy would most definitely not be gone in a year. It was four.

The age of Prophet was upon us. In fact, 1997 was the very year that Clear Channel Communications, the company we worked for (which would later become iHeart Radio), acquired Prophet Systems. This digital audio storage and playback company would indeed render many a shift, if not entire positions, obsolete. Survivalist that he was, and continues to be, Beck saw the only way of remaining integral to the company was if we were a syndicated show. While the others would be reduced to pretaping their five-hour shifts in advance, in less than an hour (thus, quite a change in salary), only to load it into Prophet and be long gone from the studio by the time the whole thing aired, you couldn't do that to a show that was airing in a dozen markets, if not considerably more, and taking callers everywhere from Columbus, Ohio, to Dallas, Texas.

I likened Prophet's digital automation technology to the stuff of *Blade Runner*, but it was very real, very much began playing its role, and was wildly innovative for its time. It allowed Clear Channel to centralize and automate its broadcasting operations across hundreds of radio stations. In other words, hundreds of layoffs. To start.

The rollout was slow, however, and Beck being prophetic (pun intended) was dismissed by pretty much everyone, myself included.

As he began promoting what would have then been the 7th Annual Stuff-A-Bus, he was intent on making it the biggest, most successful one to date. And from what I'd been told about previous years, that seemed quite the ambitious undertaking. But that's how he liked his undertakings.

In short, he'd take over the parking lot of a local supermarket, do the show live from there until every bus in the parking lot was filled to the brim with canned goods and nonperishables, even sleeping there until the whole darn thing was done. Sponsors would come from all over the state to offer up whatever was needed to pull this off and feed the hungry. Hence his getting a fairly sweet trailer for lodging. (Rumor had it, one year said trailer even had a jacuzzi.)

Stuff-A-Bus always took place the week before Thanksgiving, so frozen turkeys were a big item too, if not item numero uno. That's probably even where the use of the word "stuff" came from, but that was before my time and only just dawned on me upon writing this right now.

For the frozen turkeys, Eric Hummel, of Hummel Brothers Inc., lent a refrigerated truck. Hummel Bros. is a family business launched in 1933 when German immigrant brothers purchased a bankrupt sausage factory and began making hot dogs that would put them, and even the state, on the map. Later came red hots, hams, corned beef, and more.

Beck would do whatever it took to reach what was ultimately a self-inflicted goal. He had a penchant for dramatic storytelling, which more often than not culminated in him sobbing. One year he fasted. Whatever it took, Beck got however many school buses were stationed in that parking lot filled to the rafters with food. He'd pluck an arbitrary number of frozen turkeys he wanted from the sky and either meet, or exceed, it.

My first year as a part of it overwhelmed me, in many ways. First, there were the plentiful class trips, where we'd watch yet another school bus pull into the parking lot and dozens of first and second graders promptly get out, form a line, and conveyor belt what they'd brought into one of the official buses stationed there. Then there was the middle schooler I watched ride his bicycle from far away in the distance toward us, bags of canned goods dangling from his handlebars as he wobbled closer and closer, wherein we put him right on the air and he shared that he'd been listening to us on the radio and emptied the cupboards at home for "people who don't have what I have." Lastly, there were the bikers, rolling up in droves, and handing Glenn cold hard cash. They just trusted him. One biker asked on the final day, as a frost enveloped who remained and Glenn's sleeping quarters had already been returned, "How much for you to finally go home?" Glenn gave him a figure and the guy peeled off the bills. That's a wrap.

Second, the sleeping quarters itself presented a quandary. A very real one.

As this first day of Stuff-A-Bus 1997 came to an end—and by day I mean night, as we all stayed on long after our shifts, 'til the darkness fell and long after that, with the crowded parking lot thinning until there were only two—I gathered up my things and prepared to leave.

I muttered something about having just enough time to get home and hopefully get four to five hours of much-needed sleep (despite it being a blast!) before returning to do it all over again. Glenn looked at me as if I had two heads. He was of the belief that I'd be staying there with him, in the trailer, as others had in the past, for as long as it took for him to hit the mark he wanted to hit. There'd been tales of listeners showing up in the wee hours of the morning, 3:00 a.m. money drop-offs accompanied by bags of McDonald's for the community's stalwart radio host/fundraiser. Fast food for the food driver.

For Glenn, this wasn't over until it was over. He assumed I understood that. But I'd never planned on staying there the entire time. 5:00 a.m. to 11:00 p.m. every day—sure. But, surely I could sleep in my own bed? Grab a shower? He pointed out there was a bed in the trailer, and his shower was available in his apartment, a mere few blocks from the Stuff-A-Bus site.

This had never been discussed, so I was taken by surprise. Glenn didn't think it needed to be discussed, that it was a given, so *he* was taken by surprise.

I'm not sure why I was so opposed to staying there the entire time. We'd have probably had even more of the many laughs we were having every day and made even more memories than what we were making every week. I was never a "pile into a hotel room with my buddies" kind of guy. My bed was where I recharged. (It was 1997, so it goes without saying that I had a *suh-weet* water-bed.) Glenn felt like it was an integral part of the experience, but I disembarked just the same.

The remainder of that Stuff-A-Bus went well enough, bringing in the most in cash donations, canned goods, and frozen turkeys to date. But he kept giving me digs about not staying there overnight, both on the air and off. They were not subtle and he was clearly angry with me. I didn't understand why, nor did I know what to do. I'd try the waterbed jokes and such but he wasn't having any of it. When all was said and done, and we were out of that parking lot and back in the studio, Mr. Middle Management called us into his office.

"What's the problem?" he asked. "You guys sound off."

Glenn told him that I should have been there the entire time, that 100 percent commitment to charity was a nonnegotiable, and that I came off badly by not staying there. He stressed that he was as concerned about how I came off to listeners as I was "all in" on all charitable endeavors. It was that simple.

He earnestly viewed fundraising and charity work as a duty of the radio personality. I recall wondering at the time, if only for a moment, if Glenn was just burying himself in his work, busying himself, what with the divorce and all, piling additional duties to an already demanding annual fundraiser, plus always coming up with new events to generate dollars for organizations. But it soon became clear that charity work was—and is—very much a part of being a public figure. The more localized the better. It was more stuff that was just completely lost on me, but I was glad to catch up, and catch up quick. It gets you more woven into a community than laughter ever will, plus it's "what the microphone is really for," Glenn once said. It was all over Obi-Wan and Luke. Shit—maybe even Yoda.

If only to antagonize, Mr. Middle Management dismissed every single concern of Glenn's, saying the turkey drive had gone great and that's all that mattered. What's more, he did so with a wave of his hand and a tone intended to irk the omnipresent thorn in his Top 40 morning radio side.

Glenn went from zero to 120. I sat there mute throughout the whole thing, even as it was basically caused by me, *and all about me*, wondering if these two were going to finally come to blows. Every concern Glenn voiced was met with a "it's not that big a deal" or "calm down," until Glenn finally erupted like Vesuvius. "Storyline, remember?" he said as he approached his final remarks. "Storyline, storyline, storyline! A radio show is nothing without one!"

He stormed out. I stayed behind briefly, feeling badly, yet still not entirely sure why it was that big a deal and, ultimately, what Glenn meant by "storyline" in the first place. Mr. Middle Management took a call from a record label exec, wherein he said repeatedly that Counting Crows' new single, "A Long December," was not a hit. He was seemingly as sure of that as he was me not sleeping at the annual charity event wasn't a big deal.

The next morning Glenn brought the whole sordid thing up on air, first thing. First segment of that day's show. During a commercial break he instructed me to call in to the show playing both him and his arch-nemesis, recreating the heated exchange that had happened less than twenty-four hours before. And so I did, tackling the challenging task of using two different voices to argue with each other—one on the phone and the other into the mic, bobbing, weaving, and changing hands—with Glenn completely unhinged as he shouted "storyline, storyline, storyline!"

Glenn was still laughing when he took the first phone call of the morning. "You two are a riot," the young lady said. "Is this Middle Management guy really like that? Is that what radio is really like?" We both answered her with emphatic yeses, and then she sweetly chastised me for not staying there the entire time, while conceding she too preferred her own bed and understood.

Catching his breath, Glenn looked at me intently and said my name in the soft manner that meant it was my mentor talking and not the host of the show or even my friend.

"*That's* storyline," he said.

My first full year in radio can best be described in one word: nonstop. In addition to the Jon Bon Jovi private concert, Stuff-A-Bus, the weekly "Seinfeld Watch Party," there were countless other events/appearances, some cut from some of the same cloth and others wholly unique, if not otherworldly.

The same cloth: Glenn had more "watch party" ideas. Well, one in particular: An "Ellen Watch Party," wherein Ellen DeGeneres had her character come out on her middling ABC sitcom, which

Beck rightly pronounced a pivotal moment in television history. This one got sold to a sports bar not far from the station and, well, the crowd wasn't exactly enraptured. To be fair, there weren't rows of chairs set up. The layout of the place did not lend itself to that. And wherein the "Seinfeld Watch Party" played off one huge screen, this horseshoe bar boasted twenty-three sets, thus making anything remotely communal impossible. It mattered not, as we still drew a huge crowd, and the regulars there for NHL playoffs got their channels changed back to their games by the first commercial break.

"The Puppy Episode," which is the actual title of the episode where Ellen's character, Ellen Morgan, came to terms with her sexuality, swiftly led to a decline in the show's already mediocre ratings and it was canceled quickly after that. Even so, Glenn was fascinated by Ellen's Hail Mary, if you will. After all, she knew her series was in danger and breaking ground could actually lead it to a more solid one. Beck was nothing if not a fan of taking risks, plus the president of the Flouting Convention Fan Club.

Beck's take on the episode the following morning was sprawling, sympathetic, a tad critical (from an execution standpoint), but ultimately supportive. Yes, supportive. He admired her courage, the ground that was being broken while a door simultaneously kicked open, and, most important of all, that she wielded her TV show as a weapon. Beck did the same with his show. The difference here, of course, was that DeGeneres's play required a slew of execs to sign off on what she was doing, to back her should there be an advertiser backlash, a show of unity; Beck would just do as he pleased and answer for it later.

The main reason I share this '90s moment has less to do with a sign of the times than it does me trying to convey where Beck was at during this phase of his life. He was not a far right, hardcore Republican. For my money, he still isn't to this day. But, back in the late '90's Beck, ponytail freshly shorn but still rocking a hippie vibe, took stories as they came. Did he "lean" right?

Abso-freaking-lutely. Could he occasionally wobble to the left? Yup. (Anyone who tells you your early thirties aren't still formative years is either lying or their personal evolution screeched to a halt upon waving their high school diploma in the air toward classmates they'd never see again.)

Case in point: Ted Kaczynski's arrest and subsequent trial was another touchstone of the times. We were all over that, no doubt causing many a sleepless night for whichever PD was "overseeing" the show at the time. I feel like there might have been an overlap here. Kaczynski, aka the "Unabomber," had a reign of terror that managed to begin in 1978 and end in 1995. His nationwide mail-bombing campaign against those he believed to be advancing modern technology (Prophet anyone?) led to the longest and most expensive investigation in the history of the FBI.

Beck was fascinated by Kaczynski, particularly the mathematician end of the equation (forgive the pun), but also his off-the-grid years in a remote cabin without electricity or running water, and even some of his writings. He found him to be a compelling case study. Especially when ol' Ted declared that he was sane in court and tried but failed to fire his court-appointed lawyers due to their suggestion he plead insanity to avoid the death penalty.

The crescendo came with a heated exchange about capital punishment betwixt us. I was, and remain, pro-capital punishment. Beck, at the time anyway, was a believer in rehabilitation. Or, at the very least, of it conceptually, and dependent upon who it is we're talking about here and what they've done.

This was a broad conversation, mind you, about the death penalty in general, and it strayed from being focused on Kaczynski. I am most certainly *not* saying that Beck believed Ted Kaczynski could be rehabilitated. But he did believe that rehabilitation was a possibility and, moreover, that redemption should be on the table. I did, and, do not. His way, he ruminated aloud, was the superior option to the guillotines I so fervently wanted to be back en vogue. Which led to an En Vogue song. And then to the call to action, wherein listeners called in to choose their side. (This was obviously long before the days of #TeamGlenn or #TeamVinnie, *but* Glenn did at one point corral someone into getting a batch of T-shirts made up with both our names on them and a box directly beside them; half the shirts would have the Glenn box checked, and half would have mine.)

As for that segment, it all ended with a parody commercial whipped up right quick about the "McGillicutty Guillotine: They're all about the head."

CHAPTER SEVEN

WHO WILL SAVE YOUR SOUL?

Very early on in our time together Glenn talked Mr. Middle Management into letting me tag along to cover the Grammy's in New York. He'd be doing his show on what is known as a "Radio Row," where there is one station set up after another and after another and after another, all live on the air, and the nominees and performers and presenters are trotted through like show ponies, neighing the same answers to the same questions for as long as they can take it.

But that wouldn't be us!

Mr. Middle Management was a hard sell. He'd already cherry-picked one of the handful of people in the studio with Glenn at the time to accompany him, plus the trip necessitated an engineer. A fourth person? A fourth *hotel room*? What fresh madness is this? Will Beck's demands never cease?

Glenn knew all the right buttons to push, and he wasn't necessarily demanding it. After all, at the time, my toe was barely touching the water that is radio, but I was freelancing quasi-regularly for at least a few music zines and that gave me credibility. And Glenn leverage.

If he'd had his druthers, he wouldn't even be doing "The Glenn Beck Morning Show" live from the Grammy's. It woulda been a hard pass. This was more about a PD with his first sizable gig in the industry wanting to strut his stuff, scratch some record label backs, show management what he could do, and so on.

With me around, though, Beck would grin and bear it. That said, he for sure didn't want to do any heavy lifting, and knew I'd not only have that covered but would be happy to do it. Besides, he had done more than his fair share of "Live from the Grammy's! It's Glenn Beck!" shows. He was over it. I'd like to think he legitimately thought I'd be an asset and that the shows would otherwise be as uninformed as they were uninspired.

Mr. Middle Management caved. Or did he?

When the four of us climbed out of a limousine the radio station had bartered into our lives for the next three days, we entered the Times Square hotel to discover there were only three rooms booked. Beck went ballistic. Frantic phone calls were made. Mr. Mid clearly knew all the right buttons to push, too.

Glenn fought in vain for that fourth room and throughout it all our congenial and truly exceptional engineer kept saying to me softly "just bunk with me, man, just bunk with me. We'll have a blast." I had no doubt we would. I loved the guy from the moment I met him, plus he'd brought a big, fat joint with him that he was now threatening to withhold unless we became official roomies. Carl Osgood had done sound for some of the biggest names in rock 'n roll and even produced and mixed his fair share of records for Connecticut artists. He was beloved. The station still had the outtake on a cart of Daryl Hall repeatedly shouting Carl's name during a Hall & Oates concert for KC101, pre-Beck, which culminated with the notoriously hot-tempered Hall shouting "Fucking Carl!" for a reason no one could seem to remember. A live performance of their latest single was on another cart, and the sound is impeccable. Carl would pass away some fifteen years later, and it was as criminal as it was heartbreaking.

I felt badly declining his offer over and over, but I suffered from some serious PTSD from sharing a room with my brother in my childhood. I really wanted my own. Alas, Beck could not procure it. He came up empty-handed. Point goes to Mr. Mid.

We grabbed the keys to our three rooms and hit them one by one. Two of them were your basic hotel room, each boasting two twin beds, a bathroom and a desk for a Lilliputian, and a TV. The third room was beyond a suite. We initially thought there might have been a mistake. It was like nothing I'd ever seen up until that day. Two enormous rooms, one with an enormous bed in it, and the other the kind of room Johnny Depp was destroying on a regular basis at the time. And the TV was more like a gigantic screen folks would a decade later begin putting in there "home theaters" in affluent suburbs.

This was clearly Beck's room. Moreover, it was clearly the host of the show's room. After an awkward beat or two, and perhaps due to the squalor he had managed to spiff up and was somehow living comfortably in post-divorce, Glenn looked Mr. Middle Management's "boy" square in the eye and simply, softly, as was his custom, said, "You take it." There was no debate. There was no fuss. The guy gladly snapped up the key. Glenn turned to Carl and said "Vinnie can room with me. That way we can prepare for the show."

And that was that.

This is not, just for the record, to say that I did not pop over to that suite and enjoy the fruits of Carl's soon-to-be-labor that he had attempted to bribe me with upon check-in. Thanks to it, in fact, I wrote some really funny stuff for our Grammy show. Neither Carl nor I ever believed for even a second that he'd withhold that spliff from me.

The resulting material was funny to me and Beck anyway. And some of it to Carl. Even a little to that other guy. One person who definitely did not find any of it funny was rising folk superstar Jewel.

Being a morning show, we didn't get the artists partying until the sun came up, the ones who had just passed out as our wake-up call was being greeted by a sarcastic Beck replying *oh . . . that's just great* into the phone. None of the morning shows did. We all got whoever was hungry enough for a full day of press, had a relentless manager who was intent on doing whatever it took to break them (in every sense of the word), and the has-beens and who cares.

The three guests that we scored for our Grammy show were as diverse as one could imagine and each truly a coup in their own right.

There's the aforementioned Jewel, single number three off her twelve-times platinum debut from 1995 "Pieces of You" having just gone into a heavy rotation on KC101. That song was "Foolish Games," my personal favorite, and a knockout punch following the right and left hooks that were "Who Will Save Your Soul" and "You Were Meant For Me." She was twice-nominated for Grammys that year, in the Best Female Pop Vocal Performance and Best New Artist categories.

We also had legendary producer Clive Davis pass through, in the throes of launching both LaFace Records and—alongside none other than Sean "Puffy" Combs (his epic fall from grace decades away, and stunning in every way)—the latter birthing artists like Notorious B.I.G., Craig Mack, and Faith Evans. LaFace's roster was even more impressive: TLC, P!nk, Usher, Outkast, and Toni Braxton among them. He was on a streak. Glenn would be at his most inquisitive here.

And finally, a leather-clad Pat Boone. Oh yeah, the idol who gave my mother the number one hits "Ain't That A Shame" and "I Almost Lost My Mind" and over twenty-five other songs that cracked the Top 20. At sixty-three, Debbie's dad was promoting his new record, "In A Metal Mood: No More Mister Nice Guy." This aberration included Boone's takes on songs by artists ranging from AC/DC to Metallica, from Dio to Hendrix, from Ozzy to Judas Priest. He'd come a long way from 1957's "Pat Boone Sings Irving Berlin," 1962's "Pat Boone Reads From The Holy Bible," and his thirty-first studio album, "Pat Boone Sings Winners of the Reader's Digest Poll." You can imagine how that went. Gotta say, though, that guy was game, and his leather vest revealed a full-on gun show for a gentle soul of sixty-three.

I had written one bit in particular the night before, upon returning from the suite to catch Beck reading *American Sphinx: The Character of Thomas Jefferson*. In summation, it was a lampooning of the "Best New Artist" category. It had always appeared to me to be the kiss of death for many—if not most—artists. In fact, if you seek out its Wikipedia page it actually reads, "The award has a reputation for being given to artists whose music industry success ends up being short-lived." The jokes came fast and furious (scant years before a film franchise with that name would begin a sprawling decades-long run).

Among them: "Christopher Cross," I wrote, "won thanks to his hit 'Sailing,' which he can no longer do, as his boat has been repossessed."

I continued, "Marc Cohn won recently for his smash 'Walking In Memphis,' which is exactly what he's doing, as his car has been repossessed."

Still more: "Tracy Chapman won Best New Artist in 1989, due in large part to the single 'Fast Car,' which she no longer has, as it's been repossessed."

You get the picture.

Needless to say, I hadn't foreseen that delivering this hit list would take some balls. Artists, their managers, competitors, would all be on hand, able to hear (or overhear), potentially leading to them canceling their appearance on the show after such a wiseass bit, or their managers would pull them. Glenn, of course, couldn't care less about that, as confirmed when I expressed my nervousness. Quite the contrary. Glenn was preoccupied by something else entirely happening: the bit getting stolen by another station. I thought that unlikely, but when I'd eventually meet Scott Shannon some two years later he not only deemed that commonplace, but he also introduced me to a catchphrase he said he used often, but took no ownership of: "If you steal from me, you're stealing twice."

I did not "perform" that particular bit with my typical bombast. I lowered my voice at points, even whispering one of the preliminary punchlines, albeit theatrically. Tickled, Glenn prodded. "What's that? Speak up, Vinnie!" Ultimately, it played differently, and I was mad at myself for shrinking in the room. I'd written (what I thought were) some really funny jokes, but they needed to be delivered a certain way—with attitude. Not sheepishness. It wound up coming off . . . cute.

Anyway.

No artists overheard it, although Jewel did enter the cacophonous room midway through, which didn't help at all. The stations to our left and right did catch it, and laughed, but no thievery occurred. Not that I know of anyway. If anything, they came off as fawners. Gushers. Material like that seemed like something they wished they could do but either didn't have the nerve or were certain their PDs—who they actually respected *and* feared—would have conniption fits over. Neither show struck me as "zoo-like" and/or irreverent.

Still, when Jewel came in, the segment seeped into our interview with her. Even more stunning in person, and equipped with more than enough zingers of her own, she proved a lively interview, sparring with Beck over the state of the city (as in New York), while also telling her story of living in a van (not down by the river) before landing her record deal for the umpteenth time. If memory serves, she was with her mom.

In any event, when talk came around to her nominations, her enthusiasm was as adorable as it was palpable. She was brimming with excitement. Then Glenn, grinning with a sadistic glint in his eye, capped the interview with, "Hey, one more thing before you go. Vinnie, share your thoughts on the Best New Artist category with Jewel." Exact words.

"What're you talking about?" I managed. Again, theatrically.

"Vinnie wrote a whole thing about the Best New Artist category," he continued, feigning pride, simultaneously reaching for the sheet of paper my chicken-scratch handwriting adorned. "It's really insightful." Exact. Words.

"Cut it outtttt," I said playfully. I then proceeded to theatrically fold the sheet of paper into so many squares I rendered it the size of a Chiclet. Then I crammed it into a pocket.

Jewel simply smiled, figuring this was little more than an inside joke between two clowns and what she had to believe was a wildly small fanbase. Like Boy Scout troop small. She wasn't the least bit intrigued, and Glenn's laughter after describing for that troop what I'd just done to the sheet of paper brought us into a commercial break.

"Okay then guys," Jewel cooed, ever the "Out Of Your League" lady, "thanks for having me on." She began to leave.

I should have just let her go.

"I just want you to win the Best Female Vocal award," I told her. "You don't want Best New Artist." I don't know which was worse, the disingenuous first statement or the embarrassingly matter-of-fact second one, which happened to have been said by someone who had never won a single award in his life up until that point. Not even for Perfect Attendance or Employee of the Month during my yearlong stint in high school at the local Mickey D's. (And no one—*no one*—could take that flag down and fold it accordingly better than I alongside those epic Golden Arches!)

She tore into me. It was like one of those videos you watch where someone is innocently stroking a docile, beautiful creature, and then is suddenly mauled by it. She not only tore me a new one, she tore me a *better* one. She did that good a job. Blows like "spoken like a true non-musician" and "only someone who has never made art would say something like that" battered me from left to right. I stuttered and stammered, meager attempts to fend her off: "I actually play guitar," was one of my retorts, which makes me cringe still to this day, even at this very moment, as I type these words, Glenn's laughter reaching a pitch heretofore unheard, only making it worse. He was still laughing when we returned to the airwaves and he apprised our Boy Scout troop of what'd just transpired. Jewel cracks became a recurring thing on the show, from both Beck and the occasional regular caller. For a good, long while.

As for Clive, he thrived. Adept at the art of the interview, whether he was the one conducting one or giving one, he was slick, insightful, and even playful. He was as quick with a comeback for questions from me (such as standard radio sidekick fare like "Is there any artist you're planning on booting off one of your labels?") as he was Unclear answers given to Glenn regarding "building a brand." I swear, that's the first time the word "brand" was ever used in the manner in which we all use it—*to death*—today. Glenn wanted to know if Davis was the brand or if his roster was, if he ever worried about no longer being able to trust his ear, what he wanted his legacy to be.

He hung on every one of Clive's words. While I was still busy shaking Jewel's harsh ones off.

CHAPTER EIGHT

GETTIN' JIGGY WIT IT

Glenn pulled me aside one day to revisit the subject of charity. He stressed the importance of my affiliation with a specific one. My choice, of course. One that I might have a reason to be drawn to. If there had been any loss in my life that lent itself to one charity over another, there would be that much more heft to my being associated with it. "These types of relationships can be as good for you as it can be the organization," he said sincerely. I couldn't believe how lost that had been on me.

Catch was, I'd had no real loss in my life yet. Tragedy-free. Although, that dog I mentioned earlier on had since passed. I mentioned Cruiser, my beloved Schnauzer, who I'd actually eulogized on the air in my last official "I'm Vinnie Penn, but that's my problem." Many, at the time, believed that's what sealed the deal for me. There were scattershot laughs, but it was heavy on heartache, a bittersweet bye-bye, and the calls from animal lovers flooded our lines, many callers choking back tears.

Beck conceded that an animal charity would be a great choice but was also a popular one in radio. Had I lost a grandparent to a rare form of cancer? A childhood friend while rafting down a river with a Native American we'd just broken out of jail? It all felt fueled by the restlessness that I so came to associate with the guy. I didn't want to simply pick a charity from a hat. So I didn't. Glenn urged me to keep it in the back of my mind, though, as he felt radio and giving back went hand in hand. It was as integral to the gig as the entertaining part.

Unsurprisingly, Beck soon afterwards hatched his next charitable work, for MADD, and volunteered me as emcee. Which—I hope by now goes without saying—was just fine by me. I was the one on the show extolling the virtues of partying, the one getting all the late-night nightclub appearances, the one rolling in hungover more often than not. My involvement would carry considerably more weight. It was another extremely successful fundraiser that Glenn managed to come up with, put together, and execute in well under a month.

Afterwards, he congratulated me on a job well done. Then he pulled me aside and said, "Do yourself a favor. Buy a tux. You'll be glad you did."

We were tight, but it's Glenn and charity that's inseparable.

Glenn had also bridged the gap between advertiser and close friend with a cherubic character of a chef named Gerry Iannacone, who at the time was the chef at New Haven's #1 restaurant. In many ways, their ambitions were more closely aligned than mine and Beck's (which is probably why I have massive credit card debt, a piece of crap 2014 Subaru Forester, and they both have multiple sports cars and homes). Yes, I still dreamt of writing the great American novel, but I'd happily do that in addition to my sweet li'l gig in my hometown on the air every morning yucking it up with Glenn and playing tunes. Glenn needed the show to be much bigger than it was and had more to do beyond that, and Gerry, too, wanted a restaurant of his own, if not several.

Both of their individual goals would be reached.

Gerry was Glenn's biggest advertiser during his Top 40 run for nine years in Connecticut. As mentioned, he was a chef in the kitchen of someone else's restaurant when the seeds of their relationship were first planted. The owners requested standard-issue radio commercials upon embarking on a partnership with Glenn for their restaurant, but he did as he pleased again. They would not be pretaped sixty-second commercials, jutted clumsily in between other pretaped commercials, which were jutted in between two hit songs wherein Glenn would only play one anyway. In fact, that being the case, Glenn doing them live was the stuff of no-brainer. And they'd go far longer than sixty seconds. They were woven into the show, whatever it was we were talking about on a given morning. Storyline.

So, this restaurant located in New Haven's "Little Italy," and doing just fine with or without Glenn, found themselves getting off-the-cuff, live, epic "commercials," averaging two minutes in length. What's more, Gerry was the breakout star. Much to the chagrin of the owners. Beck peppered his rave reviews about the food, the prices, the atmosphere with references to "Chef Gerry in the kitchen," plugging in anecdotes, personalizing the entire endeavor. Revolutionizing it really. He made Chef Gerry such a reference point for the restaurant that Gerry and the owners parted ways, and Gerry opened his own place a few blocks over. He burned a bridge but built an empire. And credited Beck with pouring the foundation.

Gerry bankrolled every idea Glenn threw his way, and they could come fast and furious, born out of a local news story and not yet fully formed. The cigar dinner was one. I believe we were covering a harrowing story involving domestic violence (in between the latest songs by Sugar Ray and Sheryl Crow), and Beck simply blurted out on the air that he wanted to host a black-tie cigar dinner, with the proceeds going to organizations working with victims of domestic violence.

He basically volunteered Gerry's spatula and whisk for it. Gerry didn't hesitate. But Beck needed the biggest venue he could get, so he could sell as many tickets as possible, and Gerry was still the chef in someone else's restaurant at the time, a quaint little Italian restaurant that wouldn't cut it. No matter—he'd still commandeer the kitchen. Besides, the venues couldn't line up quick enough. Forgoing all fees, they'd be happy to be a part of something so well-intentioned. They trusted the hell out of Beck, and his countless mentions of their establishment while talking up this cigar dinner would suffice as far as payment was concerned. I remember touring the biggest of all of them, with Beck and Gerry, and it was like they spoke another language. I needed a translator. Gerry was pointing to tiny corners of the lumbering building, saying he'd put a table and chair where there was no table or chair (or, it appeared to me, even any space), thus seating that many more people. Beck was doubling down on the money making by talking about "backwards lotteries," where the winners won signed T-shirts commemorating the event.

To say it was a success is putting it mildly.

But, none of that was *storyline,* you see. These events—from the frivolous and fun to the fundraising and fantastic—were more like "very special episodes." Remember those from your favorite TV shows? Tom Hanks once starred in a "very special episode" of *Family Ties* as Alex P. Keaton's alcoholic, unemployed uncle. Very special indeed. But he'd never be mentioned in another episode of the show. He wasn't part of the show's ongoing storyline.

Everything Glenn was throwing at sales and promotions was being handled as best as they could, no matter how daunting and overwhelming. The track record was speaking for itself. It was one success after another, while the morning show was hitting an extraordinary stride. What else was Mr. Middle Management to do but make his move on Beck?

CHAPTER NINE

PRETTY FLY (FOR A WHITE GUY)

With things going so well, and Beck the happiest he'd been in years, Mr. Middle Management began slowly trying to steer the show toward one that was a more traditional Top 40 show. Lighter on gut-wrenching monologues, heavier on hit songs. Step one: more artists performing live in studio.

Providence's prodigal son was never going to earn Glenn's respect, but that didn't mean he would stop trying. Plus, he was certainly intent on trying to be Faith's golden boy (or second anyway; actually, third). Beyond that, he had record label execs he wanted to do right by, bonuses he wanted to hit, and basically a career to think about beyond KC101. He once confided in me that his plan all along had been to ultimately become the program director of the Top 40 station in his hometown, thus returning home the conquering hero; in fact, his wife and small children hadn't even moved with him to Connecticut. He was *commuting*.

When I think about the day that he worked that into a casual conversation with me—the whole "life after KC101" conversation—I can't believe I didn't see how sneaky he was being. I did enjoy our conversations about music, about what band was definitely going to be huge and which didn't necessarily have staying power. In our decidedly different opinions anyway. He seized on that moment by gifting me a pink bathrobe from the band Aerosmith, to commemorate the release of their single "Pink" off their record "Nine Lives." I was taken aback by the gesture. His "connections" impressed me, but not Beck. "Do a funny bit about the robe tomorrow on the show," he nudged. "You love music. You should talk about it more. You know your stuff."

"It's Glenn's show," I demurred. "I follow his lead."

"You can grab the steering wheel," he sneered. "He loves you."

He did. And I loved him. Further, Glenn loved music. Maybe not all of the stuff we were playing, but some of it. Alanis. Fiona Apple. Sarah McLachlan. Dude *was* Lilith Fair. It's funny; I worked with Glenn from 1997 until1999 and that traveling music festival ran that exact same span of time.

It was the boy-band slog coming at us full speed that could crush his spirit in one note, plus he couldn't differentiate between Third Eye Blind, Goo Goo Dolls, and Matchbox Twenty. Or, *couldn't be bothered to* might be a better way to put it.

"Who is this?" Beck would always ask an intern as a song was coming to an end. He'd get told and come on over the song's fading chorus sardonically declaring, "Ohhhh, that's just great." It would be dripping with such sarcasm there'd be no way even the youngest of listeners couldn't detect it. "That's The Rockafeller Skank by Fatboy Slim. So classy."

His disdain was palpable. It was also hilarious. To me anyway. Mr. Middle Management? Not so much. But I was his way in. The way to get the biggest hits of the day front and center on the morning show on a radio station that promised its listeners the biggest hits of the day all day.

"One and done." That's the phrase my employer *employed* when talking about a band who was to perform live in the studio during a show later in the week. Their debut single was a catchy little tune that we were playing often over the course of our four hours on the air every morning (it had gone from a "lower rotation"—oft-referred to as a C—to a "higher rotation"—the dream-weaving A—fairly quickly) and many a teeny-bopper was calling in to request it on route to pre-calc at the time.

However, our gifted program director could foresee the band's future. They were "one and done," i.e., one hit wonders. Despite this fact, we were to act as if they singlehandedly saved rock 'n roll when they rolled into our parking lot, celebrate the success of the single, ask about a follow-up single that our boss had already decided we wouldn't be spinning—or, at the very least, not that much anyway—and ask about future plans it was widely believed wouldn't even come to fruition.

Now, to be honest, this was his gig—to a degree anyway: Decide which band or singer had staying power and which didn't. If the guy from the band's record label wound up being one the PD got on well with, there could be some extra spins, and that could even extend to that follow-up single I mentioned, but that affection could only get the record so far.

When the performance neared, I was considerably excited. This would be a departure from how we'd been doing the morning show. We shuffled things around the studio to make room for the band, their instruments, etc. Glenn played along, especially because an in-studio performance did add a certain flourish. It made things bigger. Always bigger. Always better.

He promoted them before they arrived with genuine enthusiasm, and it was eerie how he could do such a spot-on Top 40 DJ if he wanted to. He could have made a fortune DJing weddings, except for the fact that he'd say no to more than half the requests. A guest requesting Chumbawumba would have Beck requesting they be removed.

I didn't really understand the, let's say, lack of enthusiasm about much of what we were expected to play for a long time. When we'd first met, in addition to long conversations about classic films and bestselling books, we'd have equally long conversations about the work of Billy Joel and Jackson Browne. I'd come to find out that many people in the radio business—interestingly—don't even genuinely like music, let alone love it, let alone *live* it. Mr. Middle Management merely saw it as a means to an end. It was mathematical to him. He approached it like Jonah Hill's character approached baseball players in the film *Moneyball.*

When the band—who shall remain nameless—entered the studio they couldn't have been more unassuming. You'd have walked right by 'em at a mall. Not a one of them stood out in any real way—it was band without a Paul, i.e., "The Cute One" or a George, i.e., "The Quiet One." A wave of flannel and trucker hats crashing down on the shore of what we referred to as our studio.

But they were quite nice fellows, and I noticed that they didn't bring much by way of equipment. In fact, the drummer simply flipped our recycling bin over to handle the percussion for the two songs they would be doing (the single, and the follow-up that we were already told wouldn't see more than a week's worth of spins).

Glenn's questions, your tried-and-true interview questions, were asked with as much genuine interest as he could muster. *Where are you from? How long have you been together? How are you handling fame?* They answered uniformly, each member taking a question. And then they played their songs.

I have to admit, it was a hoot watching this five-piece crammed into our studio, hammering out an acoustic version of their hit, the lead singer using the microphone directly to my right, the one that the traffic girl's spit was still freshly on. They sounded good, and the whole thing lasted less than three quarters of an hour.

That second single did come and go, and truth be told it was a better song. Fact is, this was a band that just appeared from nowhere and returned there, all while that first song was basically crammed down listeners' throats to the point that they had no choice but to assume it was a hit, thus it *became one*. There was a lot of this I was beginning to notice.

One member had brought a mandolin, though. I admired it, jokingly asking if he could play "Eruption" on it, the late Eddie Van Halen's signature guitar overture. The mandolin had caught Beck's eye, too, and he took the notion of doing a solo to the next level. He asked the guy for an impromptu instrumental on the chipped Gibson. Soon enough the guy was a-pickin' and a-grinnin'. He could really play that thing, and Glenn was wowed by his artistry. They had a nice chat after that, while Mr. Middle Management grinned from ear to ear on the outside of the studio looking in. He thought he'd scored some points with Glenn that day, but he hadn't. He'd forever be on the outside looking in.

Or, at least for the next few months.

On a side note, about fifteen years later I wound up at a festival where this band was one of the acts, and the oddest thing happened. That one "hit" was the least well received of the lot, and the crowd sang along to almost every *other* song they performed, at some points the singer and band falling silent, letting the crowd carry entire second halves of songs I'd never even heard of before, loudly and with conviction, beer cans clinking and high fives abounding. They were what radio execs would come to dismiss as "a college band."

But radio only remembers them for that one song, and not even all that well. If only that second single had been forced down people's throats, I thought to myself; if it was played once an hour every hour, like its predecessor, people in their cars or bedrooms or basements would surely believe it must be a hit too. It must be good. It had to be. It was being played on the radio constantly.

Now the coast was clear for more live performances in the studio. Some went well, others not so much. One vocalist for a glorified boy band referenced Sammy Davis Jr. as an influence and his subsequent performance was taken considerably more seriously by Beck, plus included some nice patter between them. Meanwhile, Glenn groaned as one young girl sang her hit song over a track in-studio, but powered through, even likening her vocals to that of none other than Nina Simone. The reference lost on her, Glenn could only be satiated by the promise of an egg sandwich run immediately upon them leaving.

He likened the live performances to adding a "variety show" vibe, although I couldn't recall any variety shows where the host delivered pro-life monologues or blistering takedowns about God having been taken out of the classroom. (Of note: Two of the biggest hits we were playing at the time were "One Of Us," where singer/songwriter Joan Osborne asks us to mull over if He was one of us, "just a stranger on a bus," and alt-rockers Dishwalla had their one hit with "Counting Blue Cars," with its rousing chorus of "Tell me all your thoughts on God, 'cuz I'd really love to hear them.")

Furthermore, Mr. Middle Management could only get so many performers to make a pit stop at our studio in Hamden, Connecticut, between six and ten in the morning. So, I started going local.

Again, some went well, others not so much. Of those that went well, Christine Ohlman stands out, as does a singer/songwriter living in a trailer in Long Island at the time and performing the music of Oyster Bay's own Billy Joel. He'd named his band Big Shot, and the gang from Trod Nossel asked for a personal favor in having him come in one morning to play, just him and a keyboard, with me introducing him on stage that night at his first Connecticut booking at a tiny pub in New Haven, where on one side of the street you could meet the most beautiful girl in your life, and the other you could get stabbed. This marked the first time I'd ever heard the term "tribute band," but some twenty years later there'd be hundreds, if not thousands, of them. What's more, twenty years later this singer/songwriter would be playing alongside The Piano Man himself, once Joel came out of retirement and began a residency at Madison Square Garden. To this day, Mike DelGuidice credits our show with breaking Big Shot out of Long Island, ultimately paving the way for him to work with his rock 'n roll hero, plus continue writing and recording his own stellar original material. One of his songs, "Ordinary Guy," was picked to be the theme song for *Kevin Can Wait,* the sitcom that lured Kevin James back to television after his long-running hit show *King of Queens* wrapped.

Mr. Middle Management loathed the live local music segments. He took the complaint to Faith, where it, again, fell on deaf ears. She loved it. (I suspect what she really loved was that Big Shot began selling out venues immediately, and all of those venues were either already advertisers on the radio station, or would subsequently become advertisers on the station.)

Mr. Middle's time had finally come by then, though. The job he'd waited his entire professional life for had become open and became his. His bon voyage party wound up being oddly bittersweet. For me anyway. I don't even remember Glenn attending it. He might have, but I have no memory of it. I'd exacted a rhythm with him. Both of our fathers were born and raised in Providence. We went toe-to-toe talking about music. Beyond that, I was never one for change, and I had become wildly protective of this extraordinary job that I'd lucked into. By now I was making a six-figure salary, plus had a car deal with an advertiser, and was tooling around town in a cherry red convertible. Who would want *that* boat rocked?

After what could have well been my first ever anxiety attack, it dawned on me that I was looking at it all wrong. Beck couldn't stand the guy. He had absolutely no respect for him. He Ned Flanders'd him and cast me in the lead. A new guy, who got Glenn, got Glenn's show, and didn't want to go to war every day? What was I thinking? This could be great.

I said as much to Glenn first thing the following morning. "They went backwards," he told me coolly, not looking up from the board, fiddling absently with the knobs. "They gave the job to someone who used to work here on-air and got fired."

"Really?" I countered, surprised at this unforeseen development. "Well, for Faith to bring him back, everyone must have realized he was better suited for this job."

"Vinnie!" Glenn blurted out, flustered. "It's bad. It's really, really bad."

"Okay, I believe you."

"Oh, and one more thing," Glenn said slyly just then, seconds before he was to hit the button that began "They Have No Talent," our catchy theme song with my dazzling harmonica solo. "I'm the one who fired him."

Boat rocked.

Ponytail-era Beck meeting with a young listener at a charity event.

Another day, another car giveaway.

A postcard shoot for the show, and our final promotional shoot together ever. It actually perfectly captures where both of us were at.

The long gone KC101/WELI station vehicle, with epic inflatable balloon.

I'd occasionally perform the novelty songs I debuted on the morning show, armed only with my beat-up acoustic guitar, out live with a full band. This was one of the bigger concerts, at New Haven's legendary Toad's Place. Beck would relay on the following morning's show, "I watched it and thought to myself I can't believe this is my partner."

At our annual "Green Eggs & Ham" Saint Patrick's Day event. That's me as The Cat in the Hat, although I felt as if my makeup artist in promotions made me look more like the late Brandon Lee's "The Crow." She scoffed, but the sponsor of the event's five-year-old son burst into tears upon seeing me.

Circa 2002 or so: Beck returning for Stuff-A-Bus.

Me and Twisted Sister singer-turned-radio host Dee Snider.

Jon Bon Jovi performing a private solo concert exclusively for KC101 contest winners.

Just your local morning radio team giving away a car.

At Beck's black tie cigar dinner fundraiser. I didn't get the memo.

More Cat in the Hat antics. Oh, the radio show!

Two guys and a bus to stuff.

Doing the morning show somewhere live (probably a coffeehouse) and finding the same thing amusing, which was always contagious to those in attendance.

In the long-since-scrapped mobile studio!

Debuting not just new shirts, but a new KC101 logo, created by Beck himself.

From left to right: Yours truly, "Stu" Burguiere, "Matt the News Guy," and Beck in 1999.

The whole damn radio station backstage with Jon Bon Jovi.

Me 'n Greg Brady (actor and CT resident Barry Williams).

Summer 1997. Things were just about to get crazy.

The "controversial" billboard.

From left to right: Former SNL bandmember Christine Ohlman (aka "The Beehive Queen"), me, and dentist-turned-recording studio owner Thomas "Doc" Cavalier.

A fan with a homemade banner.

Glenn thrived on doing the morning show wherever a sponsor would have us (which once included a doctor's office).

Me 'n "Working Class Dog" Rick Springfield.

A group of lovely KC101 contest winners with us in Kingston, Jamaica. Far right: A very young "Real Housewife," Dorit Lemel (Kemsley).

Glenn's cigar dinner, having corralled attendees who chose the shirt wherein they check the box for him.

Legendary Clear Channel Communications GM Faith Zila. She changed my life, and saved Glenn's.

During "Stu's Lost Weekend." The year was 2000 and the cute blonde was a new regular we called "The Astrolochick."

Beck, Jon Bon Jovi, and me. I'd be relieved of my hosting duties shortly after this picture for asking JBJ to let me hop on stage and jam with him one too many times.

Thanksgiving Eve, 2024: Me, Beck, and Chef Gerry Iannacone in the kitchen of his restaurant Encore by Goodfellas in New Haven.

Twenty-five years after our final show together, at Beck's sixtieth birthday party in New Haven, "the city of his rebirth," as he calls it.

CHAPTER TEN

SEMI-CHARMED LIFE

Mr. Middle Management's successor seemed a nice enough guy, and I got on well enough with him. He sought no confrontation with Glenn, and minimal interaction, which suited Glenn just fine. To his credit, during one of our first sit-downs he came right out and told me that one of his demands upon taking the job as Program Director of KC101 was that the morning show be let go immediately. Faith told him that this was never going to happen. "Over her dead body" I believe were the words he used in relaying the story. We'd be stepping over that carcass soon enough but until that fateful day, as far as transitions go, this one was about as smooth as one could be, considering the circumstances.

But from then on, Beck read into every move our new program director made and saw malicious intent behind each. They didn't even look like moves to me. Glenn was convinced the guy had it out for him, and me sharing what he had told me about his list of demands did little to assuage those concerns. But I couldn't keep it from him either.

Beck's divorce was still dragging on, his short-lived romance with our coworker ended in a limo en route to NYC (not even on the way back!), and I found myself telling him yet again that whatever it was he felt he had lost along the way could only—it stands to reason—be found right here, in New Haven, where he lost it.

He was on the brink of falling off the wagon, unbeknownst to me, and on the very night he was to order himself his first drink in years, at our weekly "Seinfeld Watch Party," he met the woman who'd become his second wife, Tania. They'd actually already met once, at a reverse lottery where the prize was a brand new car (said in your best Johnny Olson), and I had the pleasure of meeting her one more time after that, at the radio station. She'd stopped by to pick up concert tickets or some such—something that she'd won, and I could tell she was hoping to chat with Glenn again. Alas, she got stuck with me.

But, thanks to that second time, I roped Glenn into a conversation with her and all of her friends at that "Seinfeld Watch Party," and they never left each other's side for the remainder of the evening. Or since, really.

Beck's romance with Tania was a shot in his arm more sorely needed than I could possibly fathom at the time. For the life of me, I couldn't picture struggling with the life we were living. The show came to both of us so easily, and was so much fun, that it was truly a "four and out the door" situation. That's a radio term for doing your four-hour shift and leaving immediately upon it ending. For most program directors, it holds a negative connotation. For the good ones, it doesn't. If the show is performing well anyway, and ours sure as hell was.

The new guy didn't care that we were out of there once we were done. If anyone did, it was Glenn. He'd often tell me that the walls felt like they were closing in on him at his apartment, which I found to be melodramatic and, as such, was more dismissive than a good coworker—and, more importantly, friend—should have been.

I was often out until the wee hours of the morning, going straight in to do the morning show either from some after-hours club or woman's apartment. My relationship with Dorit slowed once she began traveling back and forth to Italy, where she had begun sowing the seeds of her fashion line. We were the very definition of "on-and-off," and when it was off I'd enjoy every perk that I couldn't believe came with the job of being a local morning show host. There were many women in my life at that time, some serious, some just seriously fun.

We suddenly began receiving memos from PD #2 urging us to focus more on pop culture. I recall one specifically suggesting we not only stay on top of Britney Spears's love life and *Melrose Place*, but to also to hit both once every hour.

Admittedly, the "once every hour" didn't even sit right with me, but *Melrose Place*? I got ya covered! Loved that show! I excitedly informed Glenn that I could take Michael and Sydney and Jane and Billy and Amanda right on off his plate. I genuinely thought this the stuff of teamwork. Not only could I do a *Melrose Place* (and, obviously, other similarly popular TV shows of the time) segment, but I offered to handle all the pop culture duties, Britney's love life included.

But Beck had more interest in Bill Clinton's love life. Much more.

The spiral having officially begun, Faith intervened much the way Mrs. Claus does in the venerable 1974 holiday classic, *The Year Without a Santa Claus*. If Beck and the new PD couldn't play nice together, she was going to have to bring in her biggest gun. In the Rankin/Bass special, that's Mother Nature. Here, it was none other than radio juggernaut Scott Shannon.

These days known as the announcer of *The Sean Hannity Show*, Shannon's been at it for so long many credit the very concept of "the morning zoo" to him, from his early '80s days on Tampa's WRBQ. Shannon was now on-air at (and program director of) WPLJ in New York City. It would also appear that, in addition to that, he was our show's "consultant." (We're about two years in to my time with Beck at this point and I didn't even know we had one of those.)

So, off to Stamford we went one night, teetering on the edge of New York, for tempura and tutelage with Scott Shannon. Our new program director voiced his concerns, Glenn voiced his, Faith acted as buffer, and I did pretty much everything except what today's hungry youth would call "networking." I said very little. He was intimidating, albeit unintentionally. He came off as a living, breathing encyclopedia. His solutions came quickly, matter-of-factly, and with a subtext of "next."

For instance, one of the bit players in the room—the newsman Beck and I had turned into a punching bag on-air—had become a problem. As the show's popularity continued to grow so, too, did his demands. He felt integral to that popularity. Whether that was true or not, he had become difficult, was pulling no-shows at station events, began demanding pay equivalent to me and even the host of the show, and just could be counted on for disruption every single morning. Lovable as he was, this was undeniable. Shannon took all of this in in the time it took for him to butter a piece of bread (I kid you not), before cutting everybody off to simply say, "fire him." He was gone in a matter of weeks.

Next.

Elsewhere, solutions came off as just as obvious, yet they were inventive. Beck wanted there to be serious content and the PD didn't. Shannon's solution: Make it a segment. Give it a name, a time it would air every day, signature music beneath it, and move on. Those who like it will be there every day, and those who don't will know how to avoid it. Further, it could be tested. We'd be able to see, thanks to the almighty Arbitron, how it was being received. We could gauge its success. Or failure.

Next.

CHAPTER ELEVEN

BUILDING A MYSTERY

As previously noted, Beck had been toying with becoming a minister and leaving radio for good when we first met some two years earlier. He was fascinated by faith, had even taken a theology class at Yale of all places, and spent the early days of his time with Tania "looking for a church." That provided exquisite fodder for our show; what hot dates those had to be early in a relationship! I'd call in to the show pretending to be her, thanking him for the trip to Harlem as part of their church tour (that was one of the actual stops), and then breaking it to him that, unfortunately, she had to leave the country abruptly, as she was a spy, or she had an ailing relative to tend to in Nova Scotia, and on and on. The more outlandish the excuse, the harder Beck would laugh. They did eventually find their church together, however, and Beck got baptized by his original Top 40 radio partner, Pat Gray, and became a Mormon.

Beck made his quest for a church a recurring segment on our show, per Scott Shannon, much to the consternation of our program director and, I was beginning to believe, even Faith (ironic as that may be, given her name). He called the new segment "The

Journey." It was an introspective, dramatic segment with a focus on spiritual alignment, following one's heart, emptiness, and the subsequent filling of that void, that was oftentimes punctuated with a story Beck would dig up in the news about people doing amazing things with the odds not in their favor, the deck stacked against them. His intention was for it to be uplifting, and it often was, but it could also come off as doomy and gloomy, and never the twain shall meet on Top 40 radio. After all, he'd cue up a Christina Aguilera or Destiny's Child song immediately following an installment. He tried to find his footing but only came away confounded. Self-flagellating. He'd ask me what I thought of the segment and I'd tell him I liked it—which I did—but something was nagging at him. Forever nagging. No one in programming complained about it to him at all. At least, not to my knowledge.

We'd get a smattering of phone calls during them. If five lines were lit up, four would be listeners utterly moved by Beck, but copping to now feeling down by the futility of it all. Life, that is.

Ah, but the fifth. The fifth was always someone who literally felt the Earth move as he spoke. Someone on the verge of calling it quits but now with a shiny new lease on life. Someone who was going to ask for a divorce that day or stop chemo that day and—thanks to Glenn Beck's "Journey"—had a complete change of heart.

Then it came to him: Beck instructed me to come up with a segment to counteract "The Journey." It was to be a complete parody of it, as over the top as can be. I was to deliver it in as melodramatic a manner as I could and create characters like the one-armed boy who every morning ate a bowl of cereal that slowly but surely wound up on the other side of the kitchen table by the time that he was done, and eventually came crashing down on the floor, his chin coated with milk. Oh, if only he could have his cereal without smashing a bowl every day! But, how? He was a lad on a mission.

This worked. Those four listeners found my segment to be the stuff of antidote, and salespeople suddenly had potential advertisers lined up to sponsor both segments. Nothing was more of a salve to radio management's bruises than sponsorship dollars.

While all of this was going on Beck had begun chiming in on meetings involving WELI, the news/talk station where I'd first started out. It had gone through an overhaul during the two years since I'd fallen into radio and now had a morning host with some name recognition in Connecticut, whose time in Connecticut had actually begun—get this—on KC101. You see the same people going up that you do on the way down.

His 1970's gimmick was that he had a "time-telling pig." He even took zany promotional photos with him. Now, here he was, back in the very building where his career began, but on the AM talk station, as opposed to the 50-watt blowtorch FM music station. Furthermore, in order to be the morning host, he'd have to pull double-duty as program director of the station. He was actually general manager of it too. Triple-duty. This type of fall from grace was commonplace. Radio was a cruel mistress, but her bed irresistible for many.

We'd have monthly meetings where we'd all gather in the conference room and start out by tackling WELI business. That'd last about five minutes. The next fifty-five minutes would be dedicated to all things KC101. But Glenn suddenly had suggestions for WELI. And they were welcome as far as the host/PD/GM was concerned, a moody fella who had prior to this shown zero affection for Glenn, and vice versa.

It began with Glenn asking if he could just say something during the WELI portion of one meeting. Stunned, that station's host, and Faith, both perked up and waved him on. Glenn opened by saying he felt something was happening with talk radio. He "felt a seismic shift coming" with regard to the format. It excited them to hear this. I was lost, as Glenn had shared none of these thoughts with me prior to going in.

In the next meeting he spent even more time discussing WELI, and even had a notebook handy, where he'd jotted down some ideas. One would be a tagline for the station that would soon adorn billboards promoting WELI that I do not believe the station had gotten at all in all my time there, and I can say with certainty would not get again for the next quarter of a century.

"We Need To Talk. Now More Than Ever. 960/WELI."

The host/PD/GM was thrilled. I remember his reaction from the first time Glenn had said those words aloud in the conference room. The guy lit up. "Ooh, I like that."

To coincide with this new direction, Glenn also launched a daily hour-long show of his own on WELI, but it wasn't "The Journey." Instead, it was called "The Impeachment of Character." He was covering the Bill Clinton scandal in real time, condemning the scoundrel on a daily basis, whilst pleading with listeners to demand better and to embrace the fact that character matters. No advertising dollars surfaced there—mostly because not one single salesperson sought to peddle a sponsorship package—but Beck's foray into talk had officially begun.

Glenn enlisted the aid of one of our show's many helpers to produce "The Impeachment of Character." Along the way we'd built quite a stable of young talent that we rotated to assist with the day-to-day for our show. Young people fresh out of college or, more often than not, high school, who wanted into radio and would happily begin as unpaid interns and work their way to an hourly wage by taking weekend shifts where they ran the board and played music but didn't say a word. Some found their way in working in promotions, setting up and breaking down the station's presence at area nightclubs or, again, car dealerships.

Glenn took a strong liking to one of them right away. His name was Steve Burgiere.

I'd met him first, at a bar appearance, when he was in promotions. He was there to hang the banners, set up the equipment, make the KC101 prize table look irresistible, and I was to get on the mic a few times throughout the evening, play some trivia with the crowd, hand out prizes and announce drink specials. I was a few vodkas deep when I extended my hand and asked his name. There being a fairly good crowd for the happy hour I only heard him say "St. . . ." And Stu was born.

Glenn asked me one morning when Stu was working our show what his name was and I told him Stu. Neither of us thought twice about it. Beck didn't question if I was sure I got it right or anything. Obviously, we'd both thought it was short of Stuart I guess. I told Glenn his name was Stu and Glenn's response was, "He's very bright."

From that point on I'd occasionally overhear them in hushed tones while a song was playing discussing developments in the Middle East or the hypocrisy of Bill Clinton and his ilk. It was a no-brainer that Glenn would have Stu produce "The Impeachment of Character."

Glenn's branching out into news/talk, on the AM dial no less, garnered immediate local news coverage, from print to the local TV stations. He hit the ground running. His pathos was primed. It was an instant hit.

We still touched on the Clinton controversy on KC101 too, with various parodies I'd write and perform like "The Clinton Family," to the tune of "The Addams Family," and "Clinton Connection," to the tune of Kermit the Frog's classic "Rainbow Connection." They both brought down the house. I'd spring them on Glenn, with him having no idea what was coming his way, all of it live, always live, and I still would occasionally use a word less than palatable FCC-wise. I remember using "splooge" once and Glenn grimacing. But I had free rein as far as Glenn was concerned, and he'd take the hit if a hit did indeed come.

Glenn and Stu's prepping for the next episode of "The Impeachment of Character," which aired for an hour immediately following our show, slowly began taking place during the final hour of our show. Next up, Glenn began promoting "The Impeachment of Character" during our show, imploring listeners to switch the station over come ten a.m. and listen to "a show that really matters."

Our midday girl didn't appreciate this one bit, and she was one of Glenn's biggest fans. As a human and as a radio host. In fact, her career had begun with her being an intern on Glenn and Pat's show.

Speaking of interns: The Monica Lewinsky stuff was never-ending, and truly providing both formats with oodles of material. Glenn even brought one of my parody songs over to "Impeachment" and used it there, which puzzled our PD as much as it frustrated him. After the midday girl read Glenn the riot act for telling people to switch stations come ten a.m. he seized the opportunity to pull the plug on Glenn's talk show. That might've actually ticked her off more than Glenn doing what he'd done. She gave it to Glenn good, he apologized, she accepted it, and as far as she was concerned it was over. She sure as hell didn't want to be used or exploited by management or slow Glenn's roll; she felt like a stone the PD was sharpening the ax on that he had with Glenn.

He drew up a press release for the local papers declaring how proud everyone was of Beck and the work he'd done on this ambitious new project, but "everyone agreed" that it was ultimately interfering with "The Glenn Beck Morning Show with Vinnie Penn" and that needed to be the priority.

The PD at WELI was equally as ticked as our midday girl, as he felt the decision on what shows come and go on his station was his call. He'd been high on Glenn since the "we need to talk now more than ever" breakthrough in the conference room, and was also a fan of the show Glenn had created. In just a few years time, in fact, he'd be one of Glenn's first affiliates when "The Glenn Beck Program" went into syndication.

In the meantime, speaking of "The Glenn Beck Morning Show with Vinnie Penn," that was about to change, too. Literally. The PD's next move would be the straw that broke the Beck's back.

And it would take Stu a full year before he one day confided in Glenn that his name was actually Steve.

CHAPTER TWELVE

GENIE IN A BOTTLE

They thought they'd nipped Glenn's talk inclination in the bud. That thought, like so many other things with Glenn actually had proven to be over the years, that it was just something he needed to get out of his system, had become perfunctory. Rote. Incorrect. Like when he wanted to program the music on the station and lost interest in that as quickly as people had lost interest in trying to understand going from Nirvana to Coolio.

But they were wrong. Further, it was already too late. Itch scratched, sure, but those fingernails sang across it. Talk was where Beck not only wanted to be, and needed to be, but where he was certain God wanted him to be.

What's more, while he was embarrassed by this development, especially given the fact that the local newspaper went ahead and run a story on it, he'd run tape on all the talk stuff he'd done thus far, "Journey" included, and had been frantically making and sending out demos. They'd even include tidbits from our show, as it so often blurred the line between zoo and talk. He had some major players in the biz intrigued by what he was doing straightaway, largely unbeknownst to me at the time. It shouldn't have mattered that the local manager of a station in a market that didn't even crack the Top 100 found his foray into talk unlistenable and reeking of high drama and fear mongering. Not in the big scheme of things anyway. But, for whatever reason, it mattered to Beck.

"Can you tell I'm gone?" he asked me early one morning, one break deep into the show.

"Whaddaya mean?" I countered.

"Nothing," he sighed. Then, after a beat: "It's just, my ex-wife used to catch me just sitting and staring, and she'd say 'What're you fixated on now? I'm losing you again.'"

I remember that morning so well. Those words so well. I related to her. The ex-wife I'd only met once. What I remember most of all was the expression on Glenn's face. He didn't take pride in his recurring despondence, or tenacity, or insatiability, or always on to the next thing nature. He looked as if he hated this about himself, like he wished he could be satisfied.

It is important to note that, as far as the show was concerned, he was nothing if not the consummate professional. He gave 100 percent every day. Sometimes it was 100 percent of what Shannon had described as "naval-gazing," like the morning he spent taking calls from listeners to answer the simple question "What is love?" But it was still 100 percent. And I enjoyed those shows, and that one in particular. The calls kept coming, and the answers—everything from the profound to the punchline—followed.

I also enjoyed the ones where he'd do dramatic readings of the lyrics of hit songs we were playing at the time. I would have bought his reading of Christina Aguilera's "Genie in a Bottle" on a cassingle. (Heck, maybe he performed the shit out of that particular one because his actually *had* finally been let out the bottle.)

So, no, I didn't notice him necessarily fixating or, dare I say, drifting. Or maybe I did and just deemed it melodrama. What I totally did notice, though, was him making demo tapes in the production studio next door.

Enter George Hiltzik.

One of the biggest agents in the business at the time, Hiltzik not only liked what he heard from Glenn right away, he got to work for him right away too. In an instant Glenn was filling in for Matt Drudge, himself a rising star in the conservative talk world, and himself doing the occasional fill-in for none other than the late, great Rush Limbaugh.

Glenn's moonlighting in NYC doing talk radio didn't rattle management, interestingly, and our PD was as comfortable dismissing that as he was our mockery on-air of him doing line dancing on an upcoming Saturday night, which we were to promote on the air. The station event was to be talked up by every on-air personality during their shift, but the first time out Beck and I cracked in the middle of talking about it and there was literally, I'd say, three or four full minutes of just muffled laughter from the two of us, which was then exacerbated by Stu adding in his trademark cackle, before Glenn could wrap up the mention with as much composure as he could muster. Which wasn't much. The clip—a genuinely unplanned, if not completely unprofessional, overtaking of laughter—became something listeners came to call in and request. The PD played it off as if he found it funny, if not a bit goofy, but Stu was certain he was seething. His checkmate as far as Beck was concerned was ever closer and, what's worse, it involved using me. And I had no idea whatsoever.

Meantime, Beck was exhilarated by his stints in New York and getting rave reviews from not just talk radio listeners in both New York and where we were in Connecticut, but also from our listeners. Because, of course, Glenn was promoting his shifts on air too, despite the fact that it was every bit the definition of moonlighting. It wasn't even a Clear Channel property where he was filling in! It was grounds for termination, per his contract. Just not on Faith's watch.

Sadly, her days with the company were coming to an end. And I had no idea whatsoever.

Neither did Glenn.

Neither did *she*.

But, early in 1999 something would happen that would preempt all things inner turmoil at Radio Towers Park in idyllic Hamden, Connecticut, a hop, skip, and a jump from the dingiest apartments in town, one of which Beck was still calling home.

Two twelfth graders entered their Colorado high school and opened fire on everyone and everything in sight, murdering thirteen students and one teacher. Ten of the students were gunned down in the library, where the duo then took their own lives. Twenty additional people were injured, and still another three in the midst of escaping. The Columbine massacre was the deadliest mass shooting at a K-12 school in US history until December 2012. That's when, in a cruel twist of irony, our own state of Connecticut would take the title, with the Sandy Hook tragedy.

In 1999, though, this was unheard of, and a horrific incident without precedent. This was B.C.: Before Commonplace.

Music programmers scrambled to take any song involving angry teenagers off the air. Marilyn Manson took the biggest hit, as it was rumored the perpetrators were huge fans, and possibly even listening to his music on their way to Columbine on that fateful day. The media pounced on this, had found their fall guy, and Glenn himself did see the rocker's lyrics as, at the very least, contributing.

We squared off again.

I'd been here before. A decade earlier, just as my first bylines began appearing in local newspapers and music zines, the hard rock band Judas Priest had come under fire from families who claimed the band's music contained subliminal messages encouraging suicide. I wasn't some huge Priest fan, but I was surely screaming for vengeance. Ancient congressmen testified that they could hear these messages and were ripe for ridicule. One was incorporated into a spot for MTV and played on a loop, entertaining an entire generation, much the same way "from you alright? I learned it by watching you" had entertained one. Maybe even the same one.

Glenn didn't care for subliminal though. He didn't blame Manson for burying messages; his take was that it was all right there in the lyrics. While I maintained that music—heavy metal, grunge, and alt-rock, in particular—was the most desperate of scapegoats, he dug in. I told him I grew up listening to all sorts of songs that were scrutinized for their lyrical content, Ozzy Osborne's "Suicide Solution" among them, but that "grown-ups" completely missed the point of that song and, what's more, even a song quite literally urging violence was a cop-out for the cops, when it came to assigning blame. The unhinged might have a soundtrack, but they're first and foremost unhinged.

Hell, if we wanted to talk about music that was full-on battle cry, we need not look further than Rage Against the Machine or N.W.A.

Beck countered by reciting a Manson song's lyrics on-air, with no tongue planted anywhere near his cheek. He selected what simply had to be the top "first dance" song at weddings in 1994: "Cake and Sodomy." I'd never even heard the tune before. I was busy digging on Manson's "Beautiful People" or their cover of the Eurythmics' classic "Sweet Dreams." This was rough.

Many of the lyrics couldn't even be said on the air, but Beck did manage to rattle off some that contained decidedly non-Top 40-friendly words such as redneck, date rape, and dick. And those were all in proximity to Manson referencing God. Plus, there was a jubilant chorus referring to white trash and the titular cake and sodomy.

I had to admit it was a long ways from Ozzy's refrain in "Suicide Solution" involving wine and whiskey.

Glenn moved on from Manson fast enough, sinking his teeth moreover into Godlessness. God, he felt, was being eradicated from our school, and prayer from everywhere that had otherwise always begun with a communal "Our Father." Here we were in total agreement. Off air he did confide that he felt it made for better radio when we disagreed, and he was probably right, but I felt we were infinitely more entertaining when in agreement. In any event, I had already demonstrated in the past that I was a bad actor.

Besides, I'd been raised Catholic. I attended Catholic school for sixteen years and even had a short stint as an altar boy. I was just—easily—the worst altar boy in the history of altar boys, and I was taken off the schedule after maybe three Masses. If I recall correctly, the priest at my parish had told another altar boy that "all Vinnie has to do is bring over the wine and every time I turn around, he isn't there. And I even ring a bell!"

Catholic church scandal aside, my Catholic schoolboy memories remain pristine, and I agreed that God was no longer welcome in a lot of the places where He'd long since been a regular. As for Glenn, he was midway through his spiritual journey, and Columbine only clinched it.

Management was miffed. Again. This time they felt they stood on considerably firmer ground, however. The story involving the unarmed twenty-one-year-old Black man had been a local story, and Glenn reminded them of that at every turn. "This is a local story! It happened right here, in our own backyard! We have an obligation!" That always silenced them.

Columbine was most definitely not our backyard. Furthermore, Glenn going off on a tear about the police was one thing; about God was something else entirely. We had listeners of all different faiths, and many no doubt with none at all, plus these monologues were less fist-pounding, more sign of the cross, less take it to the streets, more get on your knees. And then we'd play "Livin' la Vida Loca."

Beck's search for a church, as mentioned, had gone into overdrive in 1999. In retrospect, that would have been a great name for a regular segment: *"Glenn Beck's Search For A Church." This time around, Glenn pops into a Presbyterian church on the Hudson. Glenn and gal pal Tania continue their quest for the kingdom. Will they find it at First Presbyterian Church of Hudson, New York? This episode's special guest is high profile Presbyterian Katie Couric!*

His sense of humor remained intact as far as this all being fodder for the show (after all, *storyline*), but the urgency had become palpable. Tania, who had been a devout Catholic her entire life, and had attended the all-girl Catholic high school quite literally up the street from the radio station (our upbringings were quite similar, even down to us being one of four siblings in our mutual homes), had her work cut out for her. Her parents took not just their faith seriously, but also their standing in the community. That said, she was never anything but all in when it came to Glenn. I'd tease her about this quest, she'd laugh, and then she'd get deadly serious relaying to me the beautiful service they'd taken in or how much joy they could actually feel in that week's house of worship.

It was by now a constant state of urgent: his search for the right spiritual fit, for the right radio one, for a place where he and Tania could begin their life together.

Admittedly, I didn't take the radio one all that seriously. I viewed his relationship as nothing short of an anchor as far as Connecticut was concerned—this was not a young lady who would want to move away from her family—plus we were making a whole lot of money and doing so simply by having fun for four hours every morning. To me it was that simple. I began to view Beck as addicted to melodrama, and maybe even some of it was simply theater. For the sake of the show.

I, of course, was wrong. But as of early 1999 I'd have argued with you until I was blue in the face about Beck seriously wanting to leave a life that by this point was the best I'd seen it since first meeting him in 1996. That said, I wasn't delivering the "if you lost it here, you'll find it here" line anymore, every time it felt like it had just been cued up. That damn line was becoming my "whatchu talking about, Willis," and I couldn't muster the conviction to say it anymore. In my opinion, he had indeed found it here. It was me. It was Tania. It was this show.

Again, I, of course, was wrong.

Now, what didn't help all of this swirling urgency were our intermittent jaunts to tropical resorts to do the radio show live—with prize-winning listeners in tow—twice a year.

Glenn was never a fan of this. Years later he'd do his groundbreaking talk show *The Glenn Beck Program* from CPAC or the Washington Monument, and rabidly excited would be an understatement. But on a beach with sand as white as snow, with bikini-clad listeners surrounding us? Ewwww.

In fact, we'd just done our show live from the grand opening of the Atlantis Paradise Resort in the Bahamas in December. It officially opened on December 12, and we were there just a few days later, while Michael Jackson himself still remained on the property. Rumors swirled that Leonardo DiCaprio was there our entire stay. I roomed two doors down from Ian Ziering, of *Beverly Hills, 90210* fame. I tried to no avail to get him to get up early enough one morning to do the show, but despite a decade of no doubt significantly earlier call times on Aaron Spelling's dime, he scoffed at the mention of waking up before the sun came up to do a show he'd never even heard of. And Ziering is from Connecticut! I'd knock at the door and do my best Dylan McKay, and he would crack up at it. But Steve Sanders was at the Atlantis to party, plain and simple.

Glenn—not so much. He never thought doing the show from an island for a week was beneficial to listeners back home. Beck was hip to FOMO before the acronym was born. His argument made a lot of sense too, even if Faith would counter his with hers, which basically translated to, "FOMO is *exactly* what we want." Her logic was, if you're not listening, this is what you're missing out on. You could have won a trip here with us! Both made valid points, and I have to admit I came to love them. That said, if they went away that'd be just fine by me. By this point I was making more than enough money to vacation anywhere I'd like and was doing just that.

Beck's displeasure with island-hopping increased in direct proportion to how much more often we began doing it. Much of that had to do with his blossoming relationship with Tania, and also with the fact that his two daughters were getting older and it was getting increasingly difficult for him to keep disappearing from their lives. Especially for poolside broadcasts where we gave away giant inflatable Bloody Marys to the most hungover guest.

The next trip really got the best of him. He spent the first half of it alone in his room, shades drawn, Vlad The Impaler trembling at the very thought of sunlight. Midway through Tania arrived, which buoyed his spirits considerably, obviously. He appeared in the distance one evening, while I was enjoying some of Jamaica's finest with Carl the Engineer, and hallucinated that a tuxedo-clad carnival barker and a beautiful blonde in what I swear was a wedding gown appeared in the distance. I was right about the tuxedo, though; Glenn had instructed Tania to bring his with her when he flew her out. But I was wrong about the wedding gown, and also incorrect when I nevertheless predicted that a wedding would take place there before we left.

But I wasn't off by much.

Our next island getaway would be our last together, forever, and Glenn didn't bring Tania along for that one. But Dorit was there, which happened to cause quite a stir.

Having just returned from what I believe was her second trip to Italy, postgrad, she was indeed laying the foundation for that clothing line of hers there. It would debut some five or six years later, in Long Island of all places, and her first collection would manage to be both ambitious and modest at the same time. It went under fairly quickly in that highly competitive industry, but a dozen years later, when she exploded on television sets across the country, in *The Real Housewives of Beverly Hills*, it would get resurrected as "Beverly Beach by Dorit," and that line would fare much better, buoyed by the success of the series and her indomitable spirit, contagious laughter, and ability to bear her fangs when need be. All while decked out in something smashing, as she was celebrated for her impeccable personal sense of style.

As I've said, her Italy back-and-forth had led to us being on-and-off, and we were decidedly off when she joined us on our broadcast in either Aruba or Turks and Caicos (ah, the '90s—how they blur). Even if nobody believed us.

Now, before you go thinking, "Why would they? You brought her on a fabulous island getaway with you!" I did not. She *won* the trip. No, seriously, she did.

We gave all those trips away one morning while doing our show live from—can you guess?—a car dealership. Tickets were hidden in the glove compartments of cars on the lot. Each person who showed up to the lot during the hours of our show (six to ten in the morning) got to pick one car. Dorit had been dragged there by a friend, initially apprehensive due to seeing me there, although every time we were "off" as opposed to "on" we got on famously. I adored Dorit. Still do. She was one-of-a-kind in her early twenties in Woodbridge, Connecticut, and she remains one-of-a-kind to this day. If she was subdued that morning and needed some convincing by her friend to go and give it a shot, it was only because we hadn't seen each other yet since her recent return from the Amalfi Coast.

Her friend popped a glove and there they were: "I've got a golden ticket!"

But, again, no one believed Dorit or me when we profusely denied it being a setup. It took the dealership owner himself stepping forward to say that he'd personally hidden the tickets in each glove compartment, long before Glenn or I or anyone else from KC101 had ever even showed up. Still, that doubt lingered. It hung over the entire trip. It lived on long after the trip. But it was the truth. We found it equal parts comical and annoying. We were telling the truth. Why wouldn't we? We were so "off" when we took that trip.

We just happened to return from it back "on."

Glenn was a big fan of Dorit, and she was probably the only girl I dated during our few years of working together who he thought was any good for me at all. She pushed me. He pushed me. She believed in me. He believed in me. It frustrated them both to no end that simply doing the morning show in my hometown was enough for me.

To that end, Glenn's patience had grown thin. He wanted bigger and better, needed bigger and better, and needed it to start addressing real world concerns, stat, shaking off the shackles of the trivial pronto.

Hiltzik had his back.

Our PD had mine. I just didn't know he did. Nor did I necessarily want him to, even if Beck's squirming was increasing in direct proportion to his wick shrinking. He'd later confide that it was on that very trip that he made the decision once and for all to full-on pursue a gig in talk radio.

Us coming back to Faith getting fired was a final straw Beck would have inhaled a line of blow through just five years earlier.

CHAPTER THIRTEEN

UNINVITED

The show itself was somehow still firing on every cylinder, despite many a Top 40 morning radio rule being broken, and Faith being unceremoniously let go while both Beck and I were on vacation. (Yes, we needed a vacation *after* a vacation, okay? We were still getting up at five every morning on that island to do our four-hour show!) Beck called me at home to tell me the news. There was so much silence during that call I could hear the chimes on his crooked balcony tinkling, which a neighbor filed a formal complaint about. Evidently chimes can be too loud.

Both of us were in shock. Me probably more so, as I saw Faith as a miracle worker and company superstar. She hit as many goals as I did bars during those years. Beck would know the intricacies, the machinations of radio that I didn't know back then, don't know much better right now, nor am I inclined to ever want to learn them. The cutthroatism, target on your back takedowns that trim budgets as much as they do morale. Faith made a lot of money for the company but she also made a lot of money, period. Meaning, her salary was sizable. The days of "we can get three people to do that job we're paying one person to do" were approaching. Salaries were getting slashed like tires in the parking lot of Glenn's apartment building. In fact, if memory serves, Beck's salary had been slashed during his most recent renegotiation, which was another straw on a wily, skittish camel's back.

I don't know that either of us ever got a straight answer as to why she was let go, although Beck—again, obviously far more in tune (pun intended) with the corporate side of an industry he'd loved since he was a little boy, and worked in since not long after that, probably had a few ideas.

Faith was inconsolable, refused to take phone calls from either of us. She loved that station. It was her child. Hell, we were either her grandchildren or what she fed her child. I kinda like the latter. She went into hiding. Disappeared. Her profile, a quarter of a century later, remains astonishingly low. She might own an antique shop on Martha's Vineyard now. The rumors were plentiful, but the love of antiques I can confirm.

In any event, the show must go on, right? Even so, I recall the ground beneath my feet suddenly not feeling nearly as solid as it once did, and Glenn's must have felt even shakier. Catch is, Glenn didn't care about that ground much anymore, considerably less so with his muse being gone.

Changes to the show went into effect immediately. Subtle but noticeable. Especially if you were *doing* the show. For starters, Glenn decided Stu would take over running the board, freeing Glenn up to be as loose as a goose as I was.

Stu ran a fairly good board, something I never learned how to do in all my years in the business (thirty as of this writing). In my defense, early on I had been urged to do so but Glenn always ran interference. He didn't want me learning any rudimentaries, as he felt it would impede my creative process. Those conversations were always interesting to watch take place. They'd be *about me* and I'd be *in the room*, but more often than not never get asked what I thought. Both PDs had brought up me learning the "basics of running a radio show," i.e., all the technical stuff, from reading the commercial log to firing the spots, to hitting a post)—the jargon is endless. But Glenn would shoot it down like a sniper from miles away, no sweat broken. They'd snicker at his impassioned reasoning—about how he wanted me as far away from a professional broadcaster as possible, as edgy as I could be for as long as I could be, and how any distractions would prevent me from coming up with a zany bit on the spot—but ultimately relent. They knew to pick their battles. Especially against a guy you almost *always* lost to.

Glenn now sat where I sat, and this did throw me off my game a bit. It actually backed up Beck's argument. Now my back was to the studio window. I found my rhythm quickly enough, despite having lost my perch of now pretty much three years and the place I probably felt I could most be 100 percent me for the first time in my life. I'd have never argued with Beck about it or fought for it. I never once, in all our time together, thought of that show as anything other than Glenn's show. Much to the chagrin of management. Even Faith! They had begun saying the show was every bit mine as it was Beck's fairly early on, but not only did I think that a slap in the guy's face, I didn't want it to be anything other than his. I had a sweet gig. He teed 'em up and I hit 'em. Early on we'd had that long conversation about our love of Abbott and Costello movies, about the importance of timing and the "straight man," and how we'd love to exact a similar rhythm. I treasured my "sidekick" gig.

The other subtle change was that Beck could come off a bit, shall we say, resigned to his fate. Not necessarily defeated, but there were definitely days that there appeared the craziest combo platter of acceptance and ambivalence. I may have secretly hoped this was in fact the case. The job was a dream one, and I often felt he lost sight of that along the way—that perhaps even being the very thing he always lamented losing—and now was seeing he got paid good money for a fun job and had found his soulmate. Angst over.

I was kidding myself, of course. But it could, on occasion, appear that way. Again, if you were in there. There were no more daily fights for his take on political stories to get wedged in between a Backstreet Boys song and the latest from Jessica Simpson. They were twice-monthly at best.

The only time he truly commandeered the show after Faith's departure in trademark Beckian style was when he enlisted the aid of his daughters to propose to Tania live on-air. The courtship was quick, to be sure, but that boy was smitten, and it was so obviously reciprocated as to elicit envy. They've truly got something special. Soon enough she'd be accompanying Beck into the production studio outside of show hours to help him finesse his talk radio demo. His audition tape. Heeding Hiltzik's orders.

Glenn was strategizing his exit and Tania was supporting him 100 percent. Wherever that took them.

It was around this time that Glenn and I were informed by our PD that our new billboard would be going up shortly and, what's more, they were changing the name of the show. It sideswiped us both, even though Glenn, while we were informed of this, was as offended as he was certain that I was already in the know of the development. I wasn't. Furthermore, I hated the idea of changing the name of the show and I hated what they'd come up with even more.

Glenn being offended came from such a monumental decision being made and him not so much as being asked how he felt about it since, after all, it was *his show*. I'd be offended too. They didn't so much as ask him to come up with a new one himself and feign entertaining it. He wasn't consulted in the slightest—only told. He was livid.

But there was no Faith anymore. There was no faith anymore.

They were changing "The Glenn Beck Morning Show with Vinnie Penn" to "The Glenn & Vinnie Morning Show." I voiced my discontentedness but Beck was too busy assembling the barrage of insults he was about to levy toward our PD. As for him, his explanation was simple: "It's shorter. That's better." This "wasn't a mouthful," he elaborated, before moving on to say how much bigger the name of the show would appear on the coming billboards all over town considering the fact that there were less words now.

In retrospect, he was probably right but, still, these many, many years later, my mind has not changed one iota that we should have at least been a part of the conversation (Glenn, in particular), and that this equal billing—plus the way he was presenting the news of it—was intended to further pummel Beck's withering patience and even self-esteem. There was nothing passive about the aggression. The guy reveled in relaying this news to a stewing Glenn in this Stu-less room. (He had news for Stu, too, but we'll get there.)

As for me, I didn't want to lose "Penn." I was hung up on the "with Vinnie Penn." I felt like I was losing my "and also starring" billing on the show. I was the "special guest star" Heather Locklear had been on *Melrose Place*. I wanted both my names in the name of the show, the first *and* the last and viewed losing Penn as losing something key to my appeal. Hell, there were—and are—hundreds of Vinnie's in New Haven County; just plug one in. This jackass, in his haste to kick a Beck already down, was turning me into Curley-Joe of "The Three Stooges," but he just laughed heartily at all of this. Because I said all of this in his office that day.

The first words to eventually come out of Glenn's mouth, however, were, "I thought you were a man."

To which our program director, now a conservative radio host himself, albeit in a small market, but living his life on a road paved by the very guy he was pushing out, replied, "Don't question my manhood, Glenn."

Beck stormed out not long thereafter, and I will forever regard that late morning, in that office, as a true turning point for us. I should have raced after him. I should have called him that afternoon. Or swung by his place. But there'd been so much less of that since he'd fallen in love, and I knew he felt I was in on the whole thing and was equal parts angry and awkward as a result.

I hated this new name of the show but didn't have a leg to stand on or a shoulder to lean on about it.

First thing the next morning, just minutes before we went on the air, Glenn apologized to me. He confirmed my suspicions and copped to *initially* thinking I knew all about it, but Tania had quickly dispelled that notion. Glenn said, "Tania's first thought was that you must hate this even more than me and that you definitely wouldn't want it."

I never forgot that. I never will.

I couldn't quite verbalize why this nipping off of my last name felt a move in the wrong direction, costly, and just plain left me cold. I had struggled to present a cohesive argument to a manager whose mind was already made up anyway. In even more retrospect, this decision probably came from someone above him. An edict punctuating an email full of edicts, as perfunctory as the morning show is long. He was just the messenger. One who loved this particular message though, which was why Glenn wanting to kill him made so much sense.

My clumsy argument was laughed off, as he continued to stress "equal billing," saying the word equal and equal over and over. We were not equals. More importantly, I didn't want to be. How was he not getting that?

Losing my last name was a staggering blow to both ego and brand. I'd soon need my brand intact, concrete, saleable, and conveyable in one sentence. Up until now it was really just, "Glenn's wild man sidekick." There'd need to be much more to it than that. Especially with there being no Glenn.

Name change notwithstanding, the show still went off fine every morning, even if Stu wasn't the wizard with the controls that Glenn was. Beck would have his desktop humming while I did the show with a notebook in one hand and the day's *USA Today* in the other. We both brought personal anecdotes in to share on the air, and the manner in which we'd do that was by springing it on the air. There were many times I'd begin sharing, ultimately, a personal story with Glenn while a song played or during a commercial break, only for him to abruptly bark "save it for the air!" He wanted honest, genuine reactions. He believed they brought with them harder laughs and that the organic nature of it all made those listening feel like they were right in the studio with us. I agreed, I loved it, and we both still do radio that way to this day.

Glenn's Journey's and stories from around the globe—when one demanded his attention—were more finessed, takes honed. How could they not be? He was a news junkie, as was Stu. If Glenn spent the weekend reading about a catastrophic earthquake in Taiwan or the creation of the Euro, he poured over that shit. He dove all the way in. As such, he was well-versed on these actual 1999 occurrences as they were playing out in real time and his thoughts on them well-formed.

I was on pop culture duty, but it's not like I came in prepared in the same manner Beck came in prepared with the world news stuff (which our PD still deemed unwelcome on a Top 40 morning radio show, but Glenn couldn't hear him over his wishing him dead). I didn't have sprawling reports on everything that went into the making of *Fight Club* or *The Blair Witch Project*, nor did I go off on tangents about the implications of such films, the subtext, the slippery slope of it all. I'd bring up the latest movie that I saw or an episode of television, relay it to Beck, and we'd go from there. Sometimes this gave way to bits, other times to a somewhat anticlimactic "I've gotta watch that."

In 1999 there was one movie that Glenn absolutely had to see, even more than me. What's more, he wanted to see it on opening day and fill the theater with listeners of our show who won tickets by tuning in. He wanted the newest movie theater in town to add an extra screening—one that coincided with the end of that day's show—and we'd fill the lobby with a live studio audience who at show's end would then march into the theater and we'd all watch together. The promotions department pronounced this notion DOA. An impossible task, especially given the fact that the movie theater was *so* new no one had any contacts there yet and the movie was such a major release.

Do you think Glenn wound up overriding them and making it happen? If your answer is no, you have not been paying attention at all.

Do you know what movie I'm referring to? Diehard Beck fans will. *Star Wars: Episode 1 – The Phantom Menace*. To this day the guy still rags on Jar Jar Binks.

We'd done screenings before, but they were brought to us, not the other way around. This was the stuff of cultural phenomenon. Would the Hollywood execs even sign off on an extra screening. In these final days before tweets and spoilers and just plain filming on your phone, yes.

The last screening we'd done was *Austin Powers 2*, which is interesting in that the first one we'd ever done together was the first of that Mike Myers trilogy, 1997's *Austin Powers: International Man of Mystery*. We packed the theater for both of those, and for days afterwards listeners would call in to the show to say that their favorite part of the collective experience was hearing both what Beck and I laughed hardest at, and the fact that we could be heard laughing more loudly than anyone else in the theater. Those movies *killed* us.

Pop culture was still a crossroad Beck and I could meet comfortably at and would often. We were still taking in the occasional movie together as well. But his wheels were in constant motion, and I began thinking it perhaps for the best. I didn't want to have to keep convincing a guy I worked with how great we had it. I began thinking, "Just find another radio guy like him, who's been at it for twenty years, and can tee 'em up for me. Someone who can appreciate this." I'd find out in record time there was no one else like him.

So, Beck brought the worldview, and I brought my stories from the dating world and covered the pop culture outside his realm of interest.

One morning I came in with the tale of a night out with a young lady and taking in a movie and grabbing some drinks and apps afterwards. I had been transfixed by the song that played over the film's closing credits, the lyrics still living rent-free in my head, the melody haunting, and told Glenn he simply had to hear it.

"Let's play it," he said matter-of-factly, right there on the air. "We'll play it when we come back," and we were off to a commercial break.

Playing it appeared the impossible feat to me, as the movie had just been released three days earlier, and the song over the end credits was so brand new as to not appear on any record ever released. At least, not yet. It hadn't been shipped to us as a single. In fact, I noted, a song from this movie had indeed hit the trades, and we'd be getting our hands on it soon enough, but that one was by a different artist, appeared over a lovemaking scene in the flick, and wasn't even in yet. These are the days before YouTube you see. Damn, man, MySpace hadn't even happened yet.

"It's ready to go," Stu suddenly announced, in record (pun intended) time, paying as much mind to my explaining the dilemma to Glenn as I had him telling me his name the night I might him.

"It can't be it," I squirmed. I was worried this green, fresh-outta-high school do-gooder was about to play some ridiculous song from long ago, the thought of the egg on our collective face cringe-inducing. But, hey, at least my egg was no longer visible to the salespeople or contest winners who'd stare at us through the window to the studio throughout the morning. The fishbowl and all.

Stu gave me a quick taste, clock ticking, huge and digital, and daunting and daring us to stutter and stammer on the daily. It was the song alright.

"How are you playing that?" I asked him, that Monday morning in the late '90s.

"Napster," he answered, grinning. "Vin, you of all people are gonna *love* it."

I didn't necessarily fall in love with Napster, as Stu had predicted, but the reason being something the guy more than ten years younger than I could have never foreseen. Even I probably wouldn't have. First of all, nothing was *ever* going to stop me from buying my new music and being able to hold it in my hands. Nothing has. To this very day. Vinyl was already in the throes of resurgence during the Age of Napster, but some twenty years later its comeback would reduce what was happening with it in 1999 to novelty. As of this writing, in fact, cassettes seem to be making a comeback, many up-and-coming artists adorning their merch tables with them, although it appears largely shtick. Automobile manufacturers couldn't possibly—it would appear—want to limit your options more: CD players followed cassette players out of the assembly line, and the assault on AM (i.e., local) radio is going on in full force. They come off as not only in bed with satellite radio, but straight-up whores for the subscription service. Or, moreover, pimps.

I digress.

Beyond my want of physical copy, my clinging to nostalgia, forsaking the '80s and '90s and all of the magic that came with it a concept wholly incomprehensible to me, the word "piracy" did not bounce off of me like a Milk Dud pelted at the back of my head whilst I talked during previews at a movie. It resonated. It just made sense. Artists would be taking a real hit here, and some of my personal favorites were immediately vocal about it, with others following suit a ways down the road, when YouTube, et al, began not only picking their pockets, but also birthing their own artists—tragic millennials who bought the whole "exposure is compensation" line of BS. (Last time I checked my kids couldn't eat exposure or wear it to school, but okay, Gen Y.)

This is all not to say that Napster didn't come in handy throughout 1999 and even 2000—the one year I'd host the show with Stu as *my* sidekick—and I lay in that bed with hypocrisy no differently than a listener of the show I'd had fun with but became really uneasy alongside around 3:00 a.m. (Matchbox Twenty nod). It was great, personally and professionally, to have new, unreleased music so readily available, but I was going to pay for it later either way.

Beck viewed Napster in a similar fashion but, as was often the case, was able to see an endgame from miles away. He could applaud a business model with the best of them (although I'm talking more, say, a MySpace or Facebook, as opposed to a Napster, where the cracks and fissures in their model were already worn to dust by 2001), but never without a cautious eye. Mark Zuckerberg was a pioneer, yes, but would he ultimately turn out to be a threat to freedom of speech, and then some? Beck was apt to bet on that, and as such his wheels were already turning on the potential of crafting similar services, with him as overseer. Catch was, he was broke, his radio career a jalopy sputtering much like Archie Andrews's on prom night, and with only his fiancée and George Hiltzik believing in him.

Stu didn't even yet. But, we'll get there.

CHAPTER FOURTEEN

OOPS! I DID IT AGAIN

Every so often, prior to interviewing someone, his or her handler would ask our program director, or us directly, not to ask specific questions. This did not happen much, but it did on occasion.

A singer or rock star, for instance, would have just recently been arrested for DUI, perhaps, and he or she wouldn't want to talk about that. Or even significantly less scandalous in the big scheme of things, an ugly, public breakup with another celeb.

This would happen every now and then with a politician, too, but the handlers wouldn't come right out and say the words. It would be "suggested" that we "stick to what" he or she was there to discuss and not "stray to the stickier terrain."

In both cases, Beck's takeaway would be, "Gotta ask those questions!"

He only directly disobeyed the request as it pertained to pop stars if he found himself even more bored during the interview than he was at its outset, despite your ol' monkey Vinnie Penn, cymbals strapped to my knees, horn in hand, doing his best to keep things lively. When he'd go there, prompting awkward silences, scattershot answers, stern looks at publicists and sometimes even diva-esque stomping out of the studio, it did always manage to generate more feedback and chatter than the interview itself—and new single, if/when there was one—was ever going to.

Glenn lives and breathes by the mantra "question authority." He's a born rulebreaker, and the line between them and lawbreakers ain't thin by any means in his book. And it isn't. He's another kind of breaker too: a ballbreaker. He definitely found it comical that someone either with a new single in heavy rotation or with hopes that it would go into heavy rotation would have the audacity to show up to be interviewed, yet expect him not to ask them about something they made headlines about, sometimes quite recently, and other times at least in the past six months or so.

He did it with a Connecticut politician once—a man who would not long thereafter land on a ticket that was seeking election into the White House. The late Joe Lieberman had been a regular on our show the entire run, his appearances probably even predating my arrival. He was an affable, playful guest on the show, always game for recording the silliest things we could drum up, and sounded so much like Willie from the old NBC hit sitcom *Alf* (which, in an almost eerie turn, had been created by a Hamden resident, the very town we were broadcasting from) he'd *play* Willie in sketches we'd record where I played Alf. And Alf still had a taste for pussycat—wink, wink—which we were certain we were sneaking by Lieberman at every turn but later came to find out we were most assuredly not.

Joe would give answers the perfect length to questions Glenn would ask him that were decidedly outside the realm of why he was visiting us in the first place, and they got on famously.

Until Lieberman's White House ambitions came within sight. The Connecticut senator was originally a Democrat, but later changed his affiliation to Independent, despite still chairing committees for the Democratic Party and even caucusing with them. In other words, his answers stopped being the perfect length. For Glenn anyway.

Glenn called him out for something during his last visit to our show, and after Lieberman gave an abbreviated response, Glenn persisted, pointing to a passage in a book that pertained to the subject at hand, sliding it toward Joe. Without so much as glancing down, Lieberman steadied his gaze on me, gently closed the book, and slid it back toward Glenn. "Say something funny, Vinnie," the late senator said in lieu of response.

Sadly, there was no punchline up my sleeve.

Red-faced (from either rage or embarrassed, it was difficult to determine), Glenn let out an elongated "Wowwww." The guy loved waffles, but not waffling. Next thing I knew a song was playing, and Lieberman was departing swiftly, never to set foot back in the studio again. At least, not while Beck was in there. Which was fine by Beck.

Once the 2000 presidential election began to take shape so, too, did Glenn's escape plan.

The post-Clinton years were ones Beck viewed as of the greatest importance, an opportunity for America to reclaim its character, find its footing again and, most importantly, its moral compass. He wasn't gonna waste 'em. So they *had* to be numbered.

When Glenn relayed this to management, I do believe he was taken aback when they pretty much agreed. Had Faith still been with the company, it might have played out differently, but she wasn't and it didn't.

The end of Glenn's time with KC101, it was announced, would come at the end of the year. Which doubled as the end of the 1990s. Which tripled as the end of the century.

Y2K would also provide considerable fodder for Glenn's final year in Top 40 radio, and while it was absolutely something that many took quite seriously and fretted over, with Beck going off on some compelling Orwellian tangents on occasion, it also served as distraction. And a fun one at that.

One of the people taking it quite seriously and obsessing over it was my late mother, who was living in Las Vegas at the time and became a regular on the show for its final year, regaling Glenn and I with tails of stockpiling the garage with cases of toilet paper in case cash registers stopped working come January 1, 2000. "How're ya gonna wipe yourself?" she asked Beck, exasperated, ratcheting it up for comedic effect, even while that garage sure as hell was jam-packed with toilet paper. She had cases of water that lasted for years afterwards too. Because, of course, nothing came of that media-hyped frenzy.

But frenzy pays the bills. Still does. Uncertainty can handle a few of them too. Still does. Glenn knew how to mine both, and well, and for laughs as much as for monologue.

Turns out, George W. Bush did, too. He was a master of soundbites in 1999, thanks in large part to Bill Clinton's impeachment and the sex scandal that led up to it. He had been critical of Clinton long before that too, due to the Clinton administration's policies in Somalia, where eighteen Americans had died several years earlier. He plugged in words that reverberated with Beck, like honor and dignity.

Clinton's VP, the hapless Al Gore, was trickier terrain for Glenn. Back then anyway. He'd get his footing some half a dozen years later, when Gore released his documentary *An Inconvenient Truth*, which prompted Beck to pen *An Inconvenient Book* hot on the heels of the film's release. The book entered *The New York Times* bestsellers list at number one and stayed on the list for seventeen weeks.

But in 1999, Glenn just couldn't take the guy seriously. Sure, the aforementioned film would score Gore an Oscar, but that was many years off. As Y2K loomed, and Gore lapped up water from its natural springs, he only managed to elicit mockery with his global warming theories and blatant distancing of himself from Clinton. The only time Glenn could take Gore seriously was when the subject of who his running mate looked to be came up. And that's because it was none other than Joe "Willie" Lieberman.

In short, 1999 proved a mish-mosh of a final year together on the air. Between Glenn's yen for talk, and management's aversion to it, there were Y2K parties being planned and also not one but two parties for Glenn: A goodbye one and a wedding.

We had good days and bad days, and good shows and bad shows. The elephant in the room that entire year sometimes dozed, but many times blared its trunk to the point of being deafening. We'd both ignore it the best we could, but there was one person in the room who wasn't afforded such a luxury: Stu.

See, for Stu, 1999 was the year management not only finally took notice of him, but also needed an answer to one question: Would he stay or would he go?

Beck's future remained uncertain all the way up to November 1999. Yes, he and KC101 were parting ways and, yes, Glenn was moving into the news/talk realm, but that doesn't mean he had a place to move to. Hiltzik was hustling him, but the fruits of that labor were a ways off from ripe.

My future was uncertain too, but I had a job: Beck's old one. From co-host to host, with few thinking that I would be able to pull it off—the same few who declared Beck's goal to be little more than becoming some sort of "Rush wannabe." That was the chatter in the halls and malls, him pulling it off possible by some, add an "im-" by others, even though Beck had moonlighted over the course of that last year doing Top 40, going into NYC to fill in for Matt Drudge, honing his talk style, which would not be far removed from his morning zoo one really. He'd made the necessary noise during those fill-ins too, gotten the requisite headlines, causing tremors in the beltway. Even so, the prevailing sentiment was that he was leaving behind a good thing, the believers few and far between.

For my money, I thought talk was an insane move. I can't say enough how much I felt like he was taking a great thing for granted and leaving a great thing behind. He'd tell me talk was about to explode and I'd reply, "Yes, yes it is!" (It would all be in the inflection; he'd laugh too, but his resolve was unshakable.)

Further, the prevailing sentiment was that he wouldn't last a minute *doing* talk. We have many a former colleague who goes about their business saying they always knew Beck was destined for greatness, and that his success in the talk format doesn't surprise them in the least bit.

They're full of it. I knew who believed and who didn't.

Personally, I didn't know if he'd sink or if he'd swim—they were different waters than the ones we'd been surfing for three years. Choppier, with a wicked undertow, no lifeguard on duty until after the drowning.

What I definitely *did* know was that I was panicked. Being Beck's sidekick was a cushy gig and I didn't want it to end. I began to resent him for his inability to get paid six figures to have some laughs and play some music. We were professional party-throwers. Two Gatsbys and a Stu. Is there a better job than that? There are worse ones, and I'd had them. He'd only had this one though, and he'd bored of it. I could see that plain as day, and I'd finally—begrudgingly—accepted it, but said acceptance did not come without some chafing.

Our small talk between breaks lessened, as did our talking on the telephone in the afternoons. But as his last day grew nearer he dropped any and all interest in doing serious monologues or covering any of the stories that he'd ordinarily be incapable of not commenting on. He was chill and silly, if a bit distracted, our final weeks together.

With me moving into the driver's seat and, what's more, Beck's buddy Stu choosing to stay behind with me, I felt confident if a bit overwhelmed. Nobody played straight man better than Beck. Nobody did "voice of reason" better. But to tell him that was to wound him. It was reductive. After all, he'd "discovered" me and post-Faith (and post haste) middle management handed him a second fiddle he wasn't keen on playing. At the same time, I was handed the steering wheel and I wasn't keen on driving.

I'd have to learn how to, though, toot sweet.

Stu would continue manning the board, but his actual driving license was literally still warm from being pressed at the DMV. He sure as hell wasn't going to be driving, though he was probably more comfortable to give that a go than I was. Ah, the eagerness of youth!

Management's decision to offer Stu the job of moving into a sidekick role, and me into a host roll, was a cop-out. And one last parting shot at Glenn. Of course, as has been aptly illustrated dozens of pages before this, that was all lost on me at the time. Sure, I viewed our PD offering it to Stu as lazy, but it also made a sort of sense. I focused on that more than the fact that it was clear he not only couldn't be bothered interviewing various potential replacements for Glenn—guys with the same amount of experience and maybe even name recognition in the industry—he also wanted to save the company a ton of money. The Clinton-era '90s excess was giving way to the "promote from within" or "eradicate that position, and add the necessary duties to someone already in the building" 2000s.

It also put Stu between a hell of a rock and a hard place. At the time the wee lad surely viewed me as the former and Glenn as the latter, only to come and quickly discover it was the other way around. I was no rock. If anything, I was a hard place.

In my defense, though, I was in one. One of the hardest of my life.

Stu vacillated between rolling the dice and leaving with Glenn, in who he'd found both father figure and mentor, to a market TBD, or staying behind with me, in the only studio he'd ever called a second home, the only state he'd ever called home, and where he was in the throes of falling in love himself. Interestingly, both Glenn and Stu found their wives during our time together.

I wasn't certain me moving into the Glenn role and Stu moving into mine would make for a great show, by *any* stretch of the imagination, but I did find great comfort in the thought of it. Stu's hands were capable ones, we'd already amassed a ton of memories together, and he'd proven himself to be hardworking, smart, and oozing likability. Most important of all, Stu reeked of demo. Glenn and me, in our mid- and early thirties respectively, were aging the fuck out. There was an actual Monday where we all shared our weekends on the air: Mine involved Dorit and I taking New York by storm, seeing a Broadway show, dining out at the newest restaurant in the theater district, and staying at the newest bon vivant hotel in the city, The W. Glenn and Tania had purchased those chimes for Glenn's patio, which came with quite an elaborate tale about the craftsman who had whittled them out of a tree chopped down in a historic district in Connecticut, thus preserving said history for all eternity. And Stu was still laughing over a movie he'd taken his new girlfriend Lisa to see on Friday night, called *American Pie*.

Yes, ultimately Stu chose me, but he was really choosing home and Lisa. And it would prove but a reprieve from Beck and his swift ascension in the talk world.

Still, that PD had pit Glenn and me against each other by offering Stu the gig and felt triumphant that he was sending the guy who'd once fired him off without his right hand. He was, as Stu had been Glenn's right-hand man for the entirety of that year, and all of his talk radio work to date.

I remember the night Stu called me to tell me he was staying and how excited he sounded. I admittedly breathed a sigh of relief myself. I didn't want the show's audience to suffer through too much change at once. He was very honest about the fact that he had initially declined but that the PD just upped the offer every time. Every no from Stu became more money from the PD. The final offer came with the guy assuring Stu he'd hold his hand through the entire transition, make sure he was comfortable, got any additional training he might feel he needed, and then some. He'd be there for him every step of the way.

That PD left the company in January of 2000, less than a month after Glenn drove his new Volkswagen out of Connecticut, destination Tampa.

CHAPTER FIFTEEN

DON'T LOOK BACK IN ANGER

As detached as he was becoming, Glenn could not for the life of him back-sell any of the Britney, Xtina, Jessica—even Mandy!—without a dissertation on the sexualization of youth. His dives got deeper during the songs about how deep the danger Top 40 was in really was; the consolidating and merging not just of the companies but all the syndication that would be borne from it. Stu and I hung on every word, but also the ones uttered by a PD whose certainty that we were here to stay was as convincing as they proved to be hollow, an empty suitcase probably propped up in the corner of his dumpster fire apartment being readied to be filled as he said them.

We also got a new general manager at this time, and we had one-on-ones where he doubled down on what the PD was saying. To me anyway. He was not a Stu fan, reducing him to a "kid that just got lucky." Nor was he a fan of Glenn, telling me that his talk career would never take off because—and here I absolutely, positively do quote—"people will see right through him." He'd soon leave his wife for another manager in the company, drench the Connecticut cluster in scandal, only to ultimately send Beck a congratulations basket when his talk show went to Number One in a year's time, and then get discarded by radio only to find a life raft in the craft beer industry.

He told me—again, exact quote here—that I "could retire right where I was." Imagine hearing that in your early thirties, making some $200K per year. He extolled the virtues of local radio, and conceded that while there sure would be some big syndication deals looming for guys with names like "Bubba The Love Sponge" and "Opie & Anthony," and even '80s rock icons trying their hands at radio like Dee Snider, that nothing ever could or would replace what I was bringing to KC101: I was born and raised in the very city where the show was broadcast. Have I said that enough?

In less than a decade Elvis Duran—whose popular New York-based morning show could already be picked up on the dial in New Haven—became KC101's flagship show.

Beck diagnosed local Top 40 radio as terminally ill. Syndication was the lifeboat, and Beck both didn't see one for him in the choppy Top 40 waters, nor did he want one in those. He saw one for talk radio, though.

So much of 1999 is a bit of a blur, in both good ways and bad, with as many exits as there were entrances, both in-studio and elsewhere in the building. We had that salesman that got taken out of the building on a stretcher. This was no longer a party—it was life or death. Sell or die. Amid the haze there was Beck, awash in uncertainty about a future that was barreling toward him, planning a wedding, drifting away. We'd be in the same studio discussing in hushed tones "the new show," yet each referring to a different one, each to different people, half-eavesdropping, half-daydreaming, all while doing a full radio show. Good ones, too.

Stu's comfort level between that rock and hard place had never changed. In fact, it'd gotten considerably less comfortable upon him deciding to stay put in Connecticut. Did Beck perceive this as his protegee not believing in him? In betrayal? I couldn't say. You'd have to ask him. Or Stu. But there was a lot there at that time, between the two of them, the three of us, in that studio in general, and an elephant getting increasingly too big for the confines of it.

Glenn approached me one day and asked me how I felt about Stu staying behind. I was as honest as could be. I'd like to think I always was with Glenn, and vice versa, but man oh man does radio breed paranoia! I told him I wasn't sure it was going to fly. Stu didn't have what it took to play the straight man, and that's what I needed and wanted. We were two sidekicks at the end of the day. Maybe a lot of morning radio shows can best be summed up that way, but I felt I was at my best as a sidekick and, more importantly, I felt like listeners of that show only wanted me as one too. They wanted to hear a grown-up talk for a bit, and then me lob a grenade in. I knew Stu to be a hard worker, a fan of the medium, and an open-minded and—when need be—outspoken voice in the room when bits and ideas and promotions and appearances were being bandied about. But the grown-up talking for a bit until I made a wisecrack? Nah. I didn't see it.

Glenn put his hand on my shoulder, maybe even gave it a squeeze, and softly but sternly said, "Tell him that. Please."

So I did.

I actually remember that call with Stu quite vividly. It was technically my first "act" as a radio show host, at spearheading anything remotely resembling professionalism, yet it was also fueled by anxiousness and naked ambition. I saw where I wanted the show to go after Beck's exit, and I did see a way for Stu and me to pull it off. Even if it wasn't the show I'd assume we'd assemble.

Stu's biggest concern was getting fired within a month of Beck being gone, which was understandable. We all felt as if Glenn was our shield in one way or another, even our protector. Sure, I never felt that he'd been called upon in that capacity for me and had even stopped feeling like I needed him in that way, but there was always a comfort in "this is Glenn's show, and he'd never let A, B, or C happen." Catch is, it was no longer going to be Glenn's show. It was going to be mine, and I, for better or worse, was considerably more of an "every man for himself" kinda guy.

I told Stu I understood that concern, coughing up no false pretense along the lines of "I'd never let it happen," as it's not like I felt I had suddenly been bestowed with some sort of power that I could wield to my heart's content. I mighta had leverage, but it's not like I'd know how to use it or feel comfortable using it. In fact, the one time I had—trying to get one of the gals from our news team a more sizable role on the show, around the time Glenn's leaving had first begun to sink in and become reality—I got *let me think about it* 'd right out the door. And she was right in there with me!

Stu continued, thinking out loud really, reiterating how the PD kept pressuring him, even letting that contagious cackle of his loose as he confided yet again, "Every time I said no he just gave me more money." I'd been there before, going in asking for a new billboard and leaving with a raise. That sorta thing. But Stu is ten years or so younger than me, had to be around twenty-two at the time, and he had a program director with a decent record in the industry making him all sorts of promises and just throwing money at him.

Plus, with each day that passed the guy was falling more and more in love with the girl who would one day be his wife. Lisa Perrone was a force of nature on the air in her own right too, having begun taking on weekend shifts and doing midday fill-ins for the station at this point. A tiny tornado of a blonde with big blue eyes and energy to match their size, she'd taken on the radio name Lisa Paige and would one day be doing mornings in Philly at the legendary station Q102. She'd go from there to mornings in New York, the number one market in radio, at the very station Howard Stern had just fled for satellite radio.

The Stu Stack was too high against Glenn. Still, Stu was nothing if not loyal, and he felt his loyalty to Glenn was being tested and this was him failing said test miserably, and its nagging at him was wearing on him. "It's ultimately your call," I said, stating the obvious, asking him what his girlfriend thought. A hometown hero in her own right, her vote was to stay. "Just know you're going to have to follow my lead. You're going to have to trust me. You can't just be the new Glenn. No one will buy that, and you couldn't be that if you tried." That washed over him, the silence deafening. I then added, "We could be dead here. But I can promise you a lot of laughs. We'll do a lot of laughing."

His guilt was abated once he managed to sync Glenn up with a friend of his, also at the start of his career in radio as a producer, who'd fill the gaping hole that Stu would be leaving.

So we had those hard laughs. For *exactly* one year. As rumors persisted that the PD who had replaced the one who'd promised Stu the world was sharpening his ax to let Stu go, Stu announced that he was leaving KC101. Effective at the end of the month.

CHAPTER SIXTEEN

CLOSING TIME

Beck didn't have a job, but he did have offers. Two, if memory serves, and neither was anything to write home about. Beck wasn't one to write home in the first place. Meaning, he felt too much time spent peering into the rearview mirror was most of it wasted.

He had an afternoon drive offer in Tampa, and I believe an afternoon drive offer in Detroit. I could be wrong about the latter, but it doesn't matter; Beck took the Tampa gig, doing news/talk, and for the least amount of money he'd maybe ever made in his career. But talk was where he wanted to be, where his constant refrain of "the future of radio" was ever louder in the KC101 studio, and remained as lost on as it was comical to me. Talk radio? You're leaving Top 40 radio, where humor and hits are king, to do eighteen-minute monologues about budget cuts, election fraud, and emerging technologies? If you say so.

He had just one thing to do before relocating to Tampa: Get married.

Tania Colonna became Tania Beck in either December 1999 or January 2000. I don't know for sure, as I wasn't invited to the wedding. I'd been there when they met, even playing the role of wingman, nudging her once to talk to him and nudging him once to talk to her. But I didn't make the wedding guest cut. Beck's Top 40 radio fatigue had begun to extend to me sometime mid-1999, when one of his morning tirades about how he couldn't "do this anymore" wasn't met with the galvanizing, mood-enhancing pep talk it otherwise always had. They were getting increasingly difficult for me to muster up. After all, I felt like I could do this forever! It was a blast. I was getting paid six figures to goof around for a few hours every morning. I'd surely gotten paid far less for doing far more—work of the backbreaking variety. I'd dug ditches. Shit, I drove a car for a medical company picking up urine and stool samples. *Shit, I drove around picking up shit.*

Beck, on the other hand, *had* been doing it forever. Or, at least, it felt that way to him. But it was pretty damn close, save for working in the family bakery as a kid. Glenn surrounded by baked goods? Not necessarily his version of hell. It was—nay, is—his version of heaven! Continuing on in Top 40 radio, that was his version of hell. My not getting that had begun driving him crazy.

To be clear, the tirades didn't happen in a weekly, or even monthly, capacity. They were far from incessant. There were one or two when Beck and I first met, before I became his co-host, and one or two midway through our three years doing morning radio together. Our final year together the frequency with which they came was ramped up though, and I began refusing to talk him back in from the ledge anymore.

As detailed here, Beck was already desperate for change when we first met. My "if you lost something here, here is the only place you'll find it" worked wonders in 1997 and 1998. But not in 1999. Besides, he had done just that: A wife. A partner. A *soulmate.* Tania was what Glenn needed to find.

His goodbye party was arranged by Faith herself, whose heart had to be broken when she was informed to leave my name off the guest list. To be fair, Beck was probably certain I'd respectfully decline. He'd have been wrong, of course, but I could totally see him being certain of that. Years later I'd even find out—if memory serves anyway—that Christine Ohlman was the band at their wedding.

All this said, our final shows together couldn't have been farther from tense or awkward. They were total free-for-alls, despite an uncertainty that hung over both our heads. Beck's need for change was gone, which enabled him to let loose and, despite my obsessing over doing a show without him to feed off of, I decided instead to relish these last few together.

When he'd gotten baptized by former partner Pat Gray, he brought it up so matter-of-factly it made for one of our best final segments together. Beck has this way of making the trivial sound potentially dangerous in ways heretofore unseen and therefore wildly serious, and something fairly serious sound like nothing. He relayed the fact that he'd gotten baptized over the weekend to me during a commercial break, and in the same tone someone would say "went to TJ Maxx and saw a movie." I burst out in laughter at his trademark nonchalance. Especially because, as I've said, Beck's nonchalance calls the craziest of places home.

We came back from a song mid-laughter, with Glenn eschewing formalities—"That's 'Slide' by Goo Goo Dolls on your home for hits, KC101"—and opening the break simply by repeatedly asking "What? What?" as he himself laughed. I'd no idea at that time how rebellious such a move was, how unorthodox. I recall how early on he once said to me that he liked for those listening to feel as if they were overhearing a conversation. I assumed many in the biz subscribed to this theory, did their shows the same way. I'd soon find out this wasn't the case, and that while there were a few that did, they would soon be extinct. They'd be Seacrested.

So I launched into how Glenn had just casually mentioned he'd gotten baptized over the weekend, as if it were akin to getting a haircut. I proceeded to ask if he was clothed at the time, ever the sophomoric sidekick. I asked if Tania had been in attendance or if, perchance, at the very last minute she had the dubious task of breaking it to him that, unfortunately, she'd been keeping something from him, for his own safety, and was entering the Witness Protection Program, or a friend of hers had been wrongly jailed, "Brokedown Palace"—style, in a foreign land, and on and on. You get the picture.

But then Beck hit me with another whopper: Tania had gotten baptized alongside him. I remember feeling like that couldn't have gone over well with her family, pillars of the community, a beloved lot, and staunch Catholics to say the least. Tania had gone to Catholic school I believe her whole life, at the very least graduating from Sacred Heart Academy, the all-girl Catholic high school next door to the radio station. Her parents were fixtures at church every Sunday. But Glenn and Tania were in all things together and that was that. If I ever envied anything about Beck at all, it was—and is—that.

Another final break of ours I recall going into enthusiastically was me bringing in my acoustic guitar, with another Adam Sandler wannabe novelty song of mine at the ready, primed not for takeoff but, rather, send-off. Some had gone over really, *really* well through the years, like "If I Were a Brady (I'd Be Peter)" and "You Don't Belong in a Thong." ('90s, remember?) This little ditty was called "There Goes My Paycheck" and was intended to be a comical ode to Beck's departure, with lyrics like "you leaving sure is scary/we'll be gone by February."

Damn, did that flop. I could blame it on the weather girl who knocked my guitar over just before it was time to perform, and as such it was a tad out of tune, but it wasn't that. The lyrics just hit way too close to home, and us being blown out by February was, we'd find out in short order, something most of the listeners thought very much a possibility. I'd hoped to sneak some sincerity into one of those stupid songs, bury my Glenn goodbye in the chorus, my thanks in the bridge, heartfelt yet humorous. Sucker landed with a thud. We all just sat around awkward afterwards, as those calls came in with concerned fans saying things like "is that really going to happen" and "that's exactly what everyone is worried about." Stu looked like he might pass out, face flush red and guzzling root beer.

So I picked that guitar back up and fumbled my way through the station's signature holiday hit "Christmas in East Haven," a morning radio abomination, written about a neighboring town and set to the tune of the Christmas classic "Silver Bells." This little ditty had accompanied my arrival in 1997, only to be immediately embraced by listeners, who went into request mode quicker than you can say "longtime listener, first time caller," which perplexed the hell out of both Beck and me. It was so "Disco Duck." So yesteryear. Glenn believed it to be beneath his listeners and I just plain thought it both hammy and corny. It was a meal! Glenn was ecstatic that I was in agreement with him about the parody basically being the SNL sketch that should get cut.

But it turned into KC101's "Hannukah Song." It's still played to this very day. Furthermore, it debuting pretty much the exact same month I did saw to it, albeit inadvertently, that I started off with a bang. Lotsa banging.

During Beck's final show on the air at KC101—his final Top 40 show ever—restaurateur Gerry showed up to give his goodbye live on the air. He'd have done so if said show were taking place in the studio, but the trek was made even easier because Beck abruptly decided that his final show would take place on the final day of his final Stuff-A-Bus. It was fitting, though.

His goodbye to Top 40 radio—especially with it taking place in Connecticut—couldn't have taken place anywhere more appropriate. It was a somber show, obviously. But probably far more somber than it should have been. It was a Top 40 radio station, after all; the very one that had given Tom Poleman his start and many others who'd gone on to greener pastures, literally and figuratively. There were uptempo pop tunes to be played, Dunkin gift cards to "blow out" (radio speak for giveaways), the precipice of the holiday season within view. Management wasn't happy with the tone, with Beck's arch-nemesis PD referring to it as a "dirge" less than an hour after the final turkey was dropped off. Beck fought back tears for most of it, but the floodgates gave way once he spotted Gerry approaching the Winnebago we were broadcasting from just before 10:00 a.m., when Beck typically signed off. He went well beyond ten that morning—to about 10:20, if memory serves—and Glenn & Gerry (of course I want it to come off like Ben & Jerry) cried, hugged, and repeatedly thanked each other for what the other had done for them.

What Beck had done for Gerry was obvious. What Gerry had done for Beck eluded some, with Gerry himself being on the top of the list. But advertisers are a radio show's life's blood, if not the entire station's. Beyond that, Gerry *believed* in him at a time when Glenn himself was struggling to do that, never mind the PD-infested waters that surrounded the studio he did his show from Mondays through Fridays for nine years. He was his first advertiser. You never forget your first. Plus, he fed him. *Well.*

Gerry's bawl-fest with Beck came off very inside joke, but neither cared. Nor should they have. Or could they have. Stuff-A-Bus always drew huge crowds, though, and many were peering through the windows of the Winnebago, watching them while listening to the enormous speakers our engineers rigged up long before the sun rose on day one, strategically placed about the parking lot so everyone could hear the broadcast at any given time. Glenn's voice cracked as he at least attempted to give a fitting introduction to Gerry, for those who might not be regular listeners and those who weren't at all, but were simply there to give. Even so, there was no way to capture the entirety of their relationship the same way you'd "hit a post" (more radio speak) whilst cuing up a song.

It was touching—for me anyway, and at least some of Glenn's longtime and die-hard listeners—to watch these two grown-ass men sob and say goodbye. But it did no doubt go on longer than it should have while, again, leaving many to look lost and visibly mouth the words "who is that?" and "what's going on?"

I remember when the first "enough" was relayed to us via an engineer, who was told by our PD to pass the message on. I had to laugh. Beck barely ever took the guy serious the year and a half he'd been on the job, and he sure as hell wasn't going to during his last show. In radio, you *don't even usually get last shows.*

After Gerry left, Glenn regained his composure, if you can call it that. He's a sensitive, sentimental soul in general; this was next level. He began a flurry of teary-eyed goodbyes and thank yous and then did something that shocked everyone inside the Winnebago with him, including myself: He asked us all to leave.

The final segment on "The Glenn Beck Morning Show" was going to be done by Glenn and Glenn alone. (Yes, it was by now called "The Glenn & Vinnie Show" but both of us hated that—even if it was at least better than Glenn's mid-80s Louisville, Kentucky, Lollapa-Zany "Captain Beck and the A-Team.")

I stood alongside everyone else, on the outside looking in, the fishbowl as it were, as Glenn delivered an extended, commercials-be-damned, oftentimes touching, oftentimes meandering, oftentimes convoluted goodbye. But he'd earned it. Hell, that shitty PD coulda bumped him to commercials any time he wanted to. He had the power, plus it was Glenn's last day, and he'd be done with him. But he didn't. Was it out of fear? Or out of respect? I always felt a little bit of each.

Beck was swarmed upon stepping out of the studio-on-wheels, greeted by unseasonably warm November air and dozens of long, loving female arms. He gave everyone their very own personable goodbye. As for me and him? Yeah, we skipped that. Was it out of frustration and resentment? Or out of an inability to articulate what each of us meant to the other?

I always felt a little bit of each.

So, off to Tampa he went, and the start was a rocky one. According to Stu anyway. Florida radio listeners had no idea what to make of this guy so keen on self-reflection, with a penchant for choking back tears. Word began getting back to me from some others that the blinds were drawn midday in the bedroom he was sharing with his bride, and not for any reason other than Beck was maybe more lost than ever and, according to these others—one of whom visited during this period, at Beck's request—dancing with depression.

Stu reported back about a segment where Glenn opined about missing his children, eschewing the news of the day (within the confines of his new news/talk format), who were back "home" in Connecticut, sharing his existential crisis with the dads out there in the same boat, of which there were no doubt many. All he received were calls from perplexed, if not belligerent, callers either asking him why he left them in the first place or simply telling him to go back to Connecticut. A Floridian "fusion of entertainment and enlightenment" was clearly a long ways off.

Meanwhile, Stu and I were off and running. This despite the fact that my way of positioning this "new version" of the KC101 morning show was botched in its execution, thanks to that nice enough yet witless PD who promised Stu the world to stay, only to leave himself inside a month. I'd come up with the bright idea of airing dramatic promos over the holiday break along the lines of "With Glenn Beck gone, you know who's in the driver's seat now! Don't miss the NEW KC101 morning show" starting on such-and-such date, and "No more Glenn means no more stopping HIM! Are you ready for the NEW KC101 morning show? Then tune in" on such-and-such date. The kicker would be that once Stu and I would start doing our new show the "who" in the driver's seat and the "him" in question would be revealed to be Stu! Get it? Funny, huh?

Not to the listeners. Especially because said PD had the station's voice guy record them with no tongue planted firmly in cheek. He'd had his tongue extracted. I put in the copy to deliver "are you ready for" quite dramatically, while the "The Stu Show!" was to come off sounding like a question, as if uncertain, incredulous even. I even stressed to the PD to make sure his intonation was comical in the reveal, and to come off as surely he was getting it wrong.

But, nope. Fans of "Glenn & Vinnie" thought Vinnie got passed over *again*, a la the ol' billboard stunt (but without a Glenn to swoop in and save the day), and they were actually getting "The Stu Show." In radio, such promos are loaded into a system with an "end date," and once that date comes to pass they stop airing. I wanted them pulled immediately. I stressed to our PD that they came out all wrong, and couldn't he hear how the tone was as far away from what I'd wanted as it could get, and on and on and on. He told me to "relax" and also—for the umpteenth time—that "radio isn't rocket science." As if I'd actually confuse the two. He was sure I was overthinking it, plus they'd only be airing for a month anyway. They hurt Stu badly. And for a smart kid—hell, often was the time when Stu was way ahead of both Glenn and me—he didn't seem to grasp the severity of the situation either.

The backlash was swift and severe, though I took the brunt of it, shielding Stu, assuring everyone who called in to call him out that it was all a joke. I ran interference on that studio phone like Glenn ran interference on Tania's friends.

I began receiving email upon email about being disrespected and that Stu was a "backstabber." He had to be receiving similar emails, but I never had the nerve to ask him, plus he sure wasn't behaving like he was. He was now sharing an apartment with his future wife, had a new car, and his head was more in the clouds than the game. Callers in to the show would even take quick pot-shots at him before answering our trivia questions, and they'd be lost on him as I rushed in to move them along to the business at hand.

It was a bad start. But, we *did* recover. Soon enough we had recurring characters and bits all our own, appearances for the show drew the same size crowds, and where Glenn did used to often have to temper my more risque material, Stu the "American Pie" fan busted a gut. I was unleashed, with raunchy being an understatement as far as much of what I began doing. Many of the hardcore Beckians would call in to announce their departure from what had become "immature and even depraved" for them, but new listeners would fill the gaping holes as quickly as they formed.

Despite only lasting a year, 2000 was a memorable one in many ways: On the career front, I began pushing my own personal envelopes, seeing just how far listeners were willing to go with me, and was delighted to discover it was a considerable length.

And on the personal front, let's just say my dance card was as full as could be.

The next PD (now my third) in line was nothing less than a bull in a china shop. He entered the building clad in a Hard Rock Café varsity jacket, a list of new rules (among them: "The on-air talent is not to interact with the sales staff"), and one lone objective: Stu had to go. I shielded Stu from this too, being the Best Beck I could be, but being the smart guy he's always been, it didn't take him long to figure out. It was often breathtaking. Besides being a bull in our li'l china shop, the guy was off his rocker. He was at ten at all times, volatile, sewn up so tight he always seemed on the verge of popping. I never saw him exhale.

We butt heads straightaway, and I learned in our very first sit-down that with this guy I'd have to pick my battles.

While he showed no interest in getting chummy with a single person in the building, he did have something to prove in the industry. He saw to it that some of the biggest names in music were calling in to the show, from Steven Tyler to Mariah Carey. Lenny Kravitz, Dave Matthews, and Third Eye Blind all performed live in-studio. The man had his contacts.

One curveball morning saw Barry Williams joining the show for the entire four hours, as a guest co-host. "Greg Brady" himself!

But the real kicker came in the form of someone who just plain played a key role in all of my early radio years: Jon Bon Jovi. He was as big a fan of Bon Jovi as I was and had as good a relationship with JBJ's handlers as my first PD, if not a significantly better one. JBJ became a regular caller, and the entire band also performed live in-studio, before a lobby full of contest winners. They'd been told they would be whisked away to a "top secret location" for the show, but the show was right here at home. They just couldn't reveal where they were. In those pre-FaceTime days this was all easily managed.

Coming off JBJ's second solo record, "Destination Anywhere," he'd since reunited with the band, and lo and behold a salivating public was waiting; first single "It's My Life" off their first record in five years, "Crush," was a bonafide hit. Now it was time for the ballad. AKA single number two.

Hence his latest call in to the show. We were on a first-name basis by this point, which was as surreal to me at the time as it is unbelievable to think back on now. Jon Bon Jovi has gone on record time and again about his affinity for the deejay, and it ain't BS. But I was still far more fan than morning man.

Here was a guy whose first two records were all over the soundtrack to my high school years and I had graduated from side-kick to host since we last spoke. I was beside myself. My intricate knowledge of his catalogue remained apparent from the outset, as did my enthusiasm about the new record. We comically settled into a patter where I would not say the name of a past hit or a new track but, rather, refer to them as "Track 3, Side Two" of such-and-such record. This amused him, and he even copped to not knowing a few that I presented that way. I name-dropped cowriters of certain songs, producers of specific tracks—the kind of stuff better served at the time on VH1's "Behind The Music" series. Top 40 listeners were probably completely lost and felt like misfits not invited to the cool kid's party. That's not good radio, and I know it. What's more, I knew it then. I just didn't care. Just like Beck wouldn't have.

I also knew that the die-hard fans of this Bon Jovi, and there were many, mostly female, and they were lighting up the phone lines, only to later praise this specific interview for years, were gob-bling it up.

I loved "Crush," even while this second single, the ballad, I felt was a tried-and-true Bon Jovi love song ("Thank You For Loving

Me") but should get bumped for another rocker off the CD considering how rowdy I was getting with my man on the air. It had to be played, though—"debuted," as it were. That's how the whole appearance was promoted. It's why he was on. As I ramped up to playing it I mentioned some of the other tunes on the disc. We went back and forth about one, in particular, which I couldn't possibly gush over more. I told him I wanted to play that instead.

His response? "If you do that, you'd be my hero." What? My hero saying I'd be *his*? Was this really happening? I looked at Stu—he grinned. He was down. If only to tick off our new boss. Catch is, it did. It made him frantic. Spastic.

He came bursting into the studio—a colossal no-no—as the bulbs from the "On Air" sign threw light down on the well-trodden carpet. He was shaking his head no, frenetically, risking rupturing veins, waving his hands haphazardly, as if pronouncing a Yankee safe at home plate. Caught off guard, I both snickered and sputtered, saying "you got it then," even while my boss was saying "you can't, you can't," spittle gathered in both corners of his mouth. Stu interjected: "Tell ya what, we'll take a break, hear from a few sponsors and *be right back*." Glenn woulda been proud.

Now I had the three minutes I'd need to convince the guy having a coronary in the studio—again, equally a huge Bon Jovi fan—how he had to let me do this now, play this "deep cut," this non-single. Hadn't we heard stories all through our childhoods, he and I, of morning radio guys deciding they preferred the B-side to the A-side, thus giving us hits from classic rock bands like Queen and Styx simply due to their gut, their ear, and their ability to do what they wanted on *their* show? Was that all urban myth? It was sure starting to look like it. I pled my case to the music lover, the Bon Jovi fan.

But the first-timer PD was who responded: "We've gotta play the new single, Vin," he said adamantly, somehow even seeming genuinely bummed to have to tell me this. He was a suit at the end of the day. Debuting the new single mattered. It was a "get."

I looked over at Stu—easily the coolest head prevailing in the room at the time. "If we just come back and intro the new song, with no mention of that other one and you wanting to play that instead, no one will know. They won't notice."

Really? Weren't they all sitting in their cars in the parking lot at their work, five minutes late now, anxiously awaiting how this would all play out?

"Seriously, they'll have forgotten," he added. "Three minutes is a long time."

Before any of that could be proven, or disproven, however, I would have to tell my hero that I wouldn't be playing track 10 after all, a rock 'n roll opus, a song with an ending that went on and on, loaded with "na na na's," tiny little guitar solos peppering the fade-out. "Captain Crash & the Beauty Queen From Mars." Bowie-esque shit. I'd have to tell him that I wasn't his hero after all. That I had no juice. Zero clout. WWBD. *What Would Beck Do*?

I knew then, and you know now: He'd have played it. Not me, though. The incongruity threw me. I came up never doing what management asked of us but now didn't feel like such dismissiveness was doable.

All I remember Jon Bon Jovi saying when I backpedaled was, "I understand." I tried to be rebel radio deejay, the guy I heard actually existed at some point in time—probably the late '70s, but he didn't bite. I guess he figured if he did it would double as biting the hand that fed him, too.

We played the new single, the ballad. (By the way, don't get me wrong—I love that song.) I sat there quietly, trying not to appear the brat, waiting out the three-minute love song. Three minutes is a *long* time.

Meantime, while "The Vinnie & Stu Morning Show" slowly but surely got its sea legs, I'd been contacted by a big shot in the New York market and offered a job at NYC's legendary WKTU. They pulled out all the stops: had a car fetch me in Connecticut and bring me out to Lake Success, New York. (How's *that* for a name?) They put me up for the night, took me out to dinner, and had me sit in on the morning show. I immediately clicked with one of the co-hosts, the super-talented, bawdy beauty, Michelle Visage. She had initially been brought in to do mornings with RuPaul, but RuPaul had fled Lake Success for big-time success in Hollywood, where the drag performer immediately began getting acting gigs. Now Visage was doing the morning show with "Hollywood" Hamilton and a stand-up comedian named Goumba Johnny. Kinda anyway. In 2000, Johnny was in the can and would be for the foreseeable future.

They offered me a fairly sweet deal—even offering to pay my first six months' living expenses—to join the show, and I was overwhelmed. It was only a few months into this new iteration of the KC101 morning show, and I'd be the second person to bail on Stu (third, really, if you count Glenn), plus he had a wild-eyed, manic maniac of a PD who was gunning for him. I declined the offer.

When Frankie Blue, the very programmer who'd taken second place KTU to the top of the market just a few years prior and was as much a gentleman as he was a legend, called me to make sure he'd heard right, I seemed only able to manage an "um" here and a "well" there. Visage was in there with him, shouting in her delicious Jersey-an way that "there's more in the world than New Haven!," when a question passed through my parted lips that hadn't yet even passed through my mind: "What happens to me when Goumba Johnny gets out of jail?" It was as if I'd just realized that a Vinnie Penn was the perfect fill-in for a Goumba Johnny.

"Well," Frankie said, calmly and coolly. "This is John's home. But if all goes well with you, and I have a hunch it will, we'll find a place for you."

So, now this was a definite pass. Goumba Johnny did get released and did return to the show, but in a few years they'd all be gone anyway. Oscar winner Whoopi Goldberg, of all people, became the morning host.

Visage and I stayed in touch for the next fifteen years or so, working together sporadically, although ultimately spending more time on the phone together than in a studio together. We'd meet in New York, where she'd have a producer lined up for the day, and a free studio at Sirius lined up too, and we'd roll tape on all manner of show—from pop culture to relationship—that she'd then pitch to people who were being pitched to death all day every day circa 2007 at Sirius. She was New York radio royalty, adored by Big Apple radio listeners and the suits, ties, and skirts deciding what they'd hear too, and we came up with a lot of great stuff. But no one ever bit. Soon she took a gig in Florida, and not long after that reunited with RuPaul to become one of the judges on that superstar's hit series "RuPaul's Drag Race." She, too, has become the star she was always destined to become, and deserves every bit of it.

In Stu's wake, a general manager arranged tryouts for several female co-hosts to work with me in the KC101 studio, even flying a few in. I kept telling him "just find me another Glenn," still of the belief that there was, at the very least, another guy out there who'd been doing radio for years and could play straight man, if not foil. This is when I truly confirmed just how one-of-a-kind the guy was; the GM—who wasn't even a fan of Glenn's—kept stressing, "there *isn't* another one."

That said, he was also hell-bent on my co-host being female. He'd come right out and say it. I wouldn't come right out and say I didn't, but I didn't. I wanted the nature of the show to remain, and in truth there was a locker room/"American Pie" mentality, even if the weather and traffic players orbiting our universe were always gals. At one point pop star Debbie Gibson and I did an entire show together and really got on well. The Long Island native was such a natural, word was management immediately made an overture to gauge any interest. Heck, Dee Snider was in "our family," doing a show on one of our stations, never leaving his Long Island home to join the others in-studio. Why not Debbie "Shake Your Love" Gibson? That idea actually excited me. Word came back that there even was interest! Alas, there was also a Broadway show on the horizon for Ms. "Electric Youth." Sigh. Two ships.

The GM ultimately foisted upon me a woman in her late twenties who was working already, living in Connecticut, and sidekicking it at a small rock station. A "29,500-watt blowtorch," I guess you could say. He really wanted a "Regis and Kelly" (now "Kelly and Mark") show in there, felt it more fitting, imploring me to not only appreciate what I'd "gotten away with all these years" but also come into my own. So I did just that, staying on at KC101 another four years.

Still, by 2001, hot on the heels of the KTU (missed) adventure, I was now a (fairly) known entity in the New York market. Another call came in one day with the 212 area code. Man, the excitement the 212 area code used to elicit thanks to caller ID coming into our lives. This time I knew the name of the guy on the other end, though, and thought it a prank. "This is Gary Dell'Abate," he announced, certain some disbelief would be expressed, and adept at navigating it. Baba Booey himself. I was about to audition for "The Howard Stern Show."

By the time I'd begun auditioning for "the Jackie chair," as they called it—the slot that had been recently vacated by longtime Stern joke writer Jackie "The Joke Man" Martling—Stu was gone, his seat already filled, and I was free and clear to take the gig were it offered to me. It ultimately went to actor/comedian Artie Lange, but not before one final, ominous tryout.

In the meantime, I'd stopped getting updates on Glenn, lest they were from the trades. I'd occasionally eye a promotional photo for Glenn's Tampa show, or a quarter-page taken out to promote something that he had coming up: Things like him reading an Edgar Allan Poe story live on Halloween morning or him broadcasting someone getting a "live abortion." (The latter wound up finding Glenn playing a clip from "The Al Franken Show" during his, after a few weeks of effective hype, capping the whole segment with the proclamation that not everyone should be on the air; this move harkened back to his days in New Haven, pre-me, when he made a bet wherein he'd walk naked across the city's crowded Green should he lose—he did, and on the scheduled day, emerged from a vehicle and a walked a dog across the Green. The dog's name? Naked. He walked Naked across the Green.)

His promotional photos really struck me though, as they were not the overly dramatic fare, him standing before an American flag flowing in the wind, peering intently into the lens before him, or clad in a jacket and tie with his glasses strategically placed atop a quasi-blurred Bible to his right. They were zany. One was Glenn caught midair, clenching a microphone like he was the lead singer of a European punk band, feet hiked up behind him. It did not convey "serious news/talk show." The Floridian "fusion of entertainment and enlightenment" era was upon them.

The next time I'd speak to Glenn was exactly one year after he left, during Stuff-A-Bus. Our first catch-up was live on the air after an entire one year had passed, and we exacted that exact same chemistry like a day had.

We stayed on the phone after his rallying cry was done, and Stu had cued up a song. (Stu would join Beck in Tampa six weeks later as his producer again, but none of us knew this at the time. Or, at least, I didn't.) I asked him how it was going and he sighed. He lamented that Floridians weren't "getting him" or what he was trying to do. I suggested he return to Top 40 (not Connecticut, but Top 40), and he told me he wished that he could.

"What does that mean?" I asked him. "Why can't you?"

"Because, Vinnie," Beck told me. "The world is about to catch fire."

The Twin Towers were felled less than a year later, the very day of my final audition for "Jackie's chair" on "The Howard Stern Show." Yep, I was broadcasting live from New York that morning.

Stern's producer called me at home on September 12 to check on me and to also inform me that while I'd had a good run, they were officially offering the gig to Lange. Beck was busy that day sowing the seeds for what would become what he coined "The 9/12 Project," seeing (and seizing) on September 12, 2001, a unity and spirit he hoped we as Americans would sustain.

In January 2002, barely three months later, Premiere Radio Networks launched his show into syndication, initially airing it nationwide on forty-seven stations.

Beck left Tampa behind for Philly, where he'd now broadcast from "the birthplace of America," from new flagship station WPHT. In half a dozen years that forty-seven would become 280.

CHAPTER SEVENTEEN

IT'S MY LIFE

In early 2015, I was contacted by someone identifying himself as part of Glenn's ever-expanding team, and let in on a little secret: They were planning a surprise fiftieth birthday show for him and were hoping to trot people who had been in Glenn's life at one time or another across a sound-stage out before him, one by one, a la *This Is Your Life*. There was the option of being flown out to Texas, where Beck had now been doing his show for a while (after a few years where he actually had returned home to Connecticut, while doing his show in New York), and put up at a fine hotel, or you could simply be whisked over to the nearest satellite station, via limousine, and brought up on an immense screen on the aforementioned sound-stage, from wherever you were in the country.

Despite the wildly generous offer, I chose the latter. It just felt to me at the time like a whole lot of running around, involving limos and airports and check-ins and so forth, for a midweek overnighter that would greatly affect my own show just so I could be a part of a show that I knew in my heart of hearts Glenn was going to detest. Plus, despite him calling in to the news/talk show I was now doing myself—on WELI no less—on occasion, we had not been face-to-face by this point in well over a decade. I wasn't sure just how warm my welcome might be. Luke at best.

I was brought into a tiny room where I had a microphone clipped on, was told where to look, and left to my devices, where I couldn't hear the Glenn birthday bash show. All I could hear was a pin drop. That pin was busy popping the balloon of the whole thing. I shoulda taken the trip to Texas I remember thinking to myself before.

"Now it's time for someone who would come to be on the same station as you in Connecticut," I suddenly heard Stu announce. "You thought your career was over. You were so right. I mean, it was totally over." Glenn can be heard giggling, seen nodding along. I could hear the giggling but not see the nodding. It's all on YouTube.

"After proving that you were the worst music program director in history, your longtime radio partner up and left." Stu thrust a thumb to his right, where Pat Gray stood, game for the whole damn thing, especially the roast aspect of the milestone. "Then came Vinnie Penn."

Audible groan. Mad muttering. *Don't overthink, Vin. In the* This Is Your Life *scheme of things you're in wasteland territory. Who knows who was just on before you and what fresh hell you're following.*

It was at this point that I could now be seen by all of them, but myself was still looking at little more than a tiny dot of light. The kind people laser onto the chest and head of teachers or performers to throw them off their game, following them around with it, terrorizing them, jutting it across their body, until said person breaks or security intervenes.

Just as game as Gray, I waved excitedly and bestowed upon Beck a term of endearment he (and, to be fair, many others) had come to roll their eyes at upon hearing: "My man!"

He laughed genuinely, greeted me quite sincerely, and yet no one can ever tell me that I was wrong: He was hating this entire show, save for the portion where his wonderful wife appeared and gave him his fiftieth birthday gift: a brand new pickup truck.

"Tell me the truth," I began, while Beck's laughter ramped up. "Halfway through that last guest it dawned on you and you whispered to Stu, 'Oh no . . . Vinnie.'" The laugh ramped up, Stu's cackle following.

"I don't think it was halfway through. It wasn't halfway through," came his quick retort. We exacted that rhythm again, baby, that same one we had so quickly established back in late 1996, in less than half a minute and all systems were go.

"Is that guest in-studio out there in Dallas?" I asked, apropos of nothing, riding rising studio laughter. "The last one? Is he there in person?" I didn't know where I was going.

"Yes," Glenn answered. "There were some people worth flying out."

Above the din of Stu's continued cackling, I exclaimed, "They offered! They offered! It didn't dawn on me at first the food that I'd be missing out on. I am now aware of the eating that I am missing. The swordfish, the porterhouses. With Stu there the root beer refills and Fritos."

"Do-ritos," corrected Stu. "Do-ritos. So, Vinnie came along, and not long after I started working with you."

"I should be Stu," I for reasons unknown blurted out. My tombstone will have the words "apropos of nothing" etched upon it.

Beck clearly took this to mean that I was saying that I felt I should have been the one still working alongside him, a Connecticut refugee, having clung tightly to those coattails, while carving my own little thing out of the massive thing he—at this time—was still in the process of building. Construction, remarkably, continuing to this day.

He might not have been wrong, but it was not a conscious thought that I had, nor was I harboring any resentment toward Stu. It's just that he was, basically, playing the role that I had played during those few KC101 years, being introduced in that same grandiose style, afforded the opportunity to hone his own voice, but now all while everyone was making some big money and snapping up photo shoot–ready Texas real estate.

Glenn was quick to defend his staunchest of allies, quickly reverting back to that initial awkwardness. "No," he said matter-of-factly. "Just . . . no."

"I mean down to the wife and everything," I continued, rambling or in the zone, take your pick. "The father of those two beautiful children. The wife, the life . . . everything," I bellowed. At this point Glenn was knee-slapping. "Stu, I miss you, and best to Lisa."

"Yeah, I really appreciate it," he deadpanned. "Come by never."

At this point Glenn couldn't hear anything, as he was belly-laughing and, in my opinion, having the most fun he'd had through this whole self-indulgent affair. Except, again, getting that pickup from his wife.

"Oh," he can be heard moaning, should you decide to dig up the video clip on YouTube. "He's so funny." Upon watching it back, I could see that it was 1997 in that moment for him. For me, too. And ya know what? It was real nice to be back there.

"I had been hearing all about this show," Stu began, ably hitting the reset button. "You two were so hilarious. But you were probably at your funniest when you'd team up on the news guy and trash his reporting. You guys tortured him. Do you keep in touch with him, Vin?"

At that time, I was still hearing from many of the folks from those early years at KC101, this gentleman among them.

"I think he hung himself," Glenn can be heard wondering aloud as Stu posed this question, panting heavily.

"Get this," I replied, "the guy's a pharmaceutical rep. That guy who caused Glenn and I to abuse Xanax is now peddling it for a living." Hell broke loose a second time. Or was it third? "Quite a statement about the pharmaceutical industry really."

"This guy," Glenn began, "we used to pound him. Like we pound Jeffy. Then we really took it to the next level, and I think he went into therapy for a very long time."

"He was a big early believer of yours," I shared with Glenn at that moment, who I'm certain still viewed his departure from KC101 as an ugly thing that left many a body in its wake. "Back when you first began moonlighting, if you will, and you were going in to New York to do fill-ins for Matt Drudge, he'd listen to all that. And he'd say to me, in no uncertain terms, 'I'm telling you, if Glenn wanted to, the show he could do!' He's a huge fan."

You can see on the clip that this touches Glenn, who had been so restless for so long toward the end of his time in Top 40 radio, he couldn't fathom there was anyone that he'd left behind who could feel this way. Surely, he'd brought them all with him.

"He believed in you far more than I did," I quickly added. It was for comedic effect. But it was also the truth.

Cut to March 2019. Beck called in to one of my fill-in shows on Boston's heritage talker, WRKO. I was by now making the rounds doing my own news/talk thing, albeit infinitesimal by comparison to Beck, yet not miles away from what we'd originally done together either. The "fusion" was the foundation.

"If you're looking for a guy to give you hope, I'm not that guy," he said, upon taking the call live, as I was mid-monologue and mid-existential crisis. Again.

"That's okay," I assured him. "You've given me hope in the past.

"This is really quite a moment for the two of us," I continued, having been made aware by him via email the night before what a fan of the radio station he was. If memory serves, why it was quite a moment for me was that I able to able to make a dream of his come true by being on it, as opposed to him always being the one to make dreams of mine come true.

Still, "Really, more for you" came his reply, chortling.

"On the one hand I want to thank you for getting me into such an incredible industry. On the other, you may not want the blame,"

I continued. It was all very Beavis and Butt-Head with big words. Maybe that's what we always were, and are.

"You are on the station right now that as a kid I dreamed of being on. There were two stations: KFMB in San Diego and WRKO in Boston. They were the dream."

"You couldn't get farther away from Boston where you lived as a kid. How were you even aware of it at that age, during pre-Internet days?"

"Because it's a legendary station. Some of us actually practiced the craft. We didn't just stumble into it and just take, take, take. And now it's my childhood dream. What, by God, is next, man? I'm just asking."

"Well, as I told you last night when I sent you that logo, I just remember seeing that at the end of so many movies as a kid: 'This is an RKO Radio Picture.' So both of our childhoods really. And now we're getting to be childish on it like it's 1999 all over again."

A rousing chorus of "I know, I know, I know" lay under every word I said, the enthusiasm thick in the air. Mine was one thing, but his? Still capable of enthusiasm being on the radio, despite being on hundreds across the country for close to two decades at this point? That's when it's in your blood. Preordained. Primordial.

"I heard you had Brad Meltzer on earlier. Isn't he great?" Glenn teed up.

"Oh yeah. He writes the kinds of books you were always toting around with you, and he writes comic books, which I'm still a collector of. When you first found out this bestselling author also wrote comic books I simply had to come to mind, didn't I? That was always a potshot of yours at me."

"N-no," Beck stammered, theatrically, his comedic timing on point. "You didn't come to mind at all. You rarely, if ever, do."

After even more laughter abated, he began, "If I'm remembering correctly, he first came to me as a comic book guy. It was about the 'Superman House,' which I'm sure you know all about?"

I admitted that I, in fact, did not.

"The two guys who came up with Superman lived in a house in Ohio. In Toledo or Columbus—I can't remember. And as they were creating the character one of them drew him on the wall. The first drawing of Superman. Well, this house was found and it was to be taken down. So they started by taking the wallpaper off and they discover these drawings. So, Brad called me—we had just become friends—and he said, 'Hey, they're gonna tear the Superman house down. We gotta save it.' So, I brought him on the air and it was the listeners that raised the money to buy the Superman house and to preserve it. That's how we first met."

"Jeez, those guys fought for so long just to be acknowledged as the creators of Superman back when we were kids."

"I actually *have* thought about you a lot with all the Marvel stuff over these years. You know I was not into comics. Not at all. I really see the power of the comic book now. It's amazing to me what Marvel has done. They were wise enough to see that those stories are universal and were going to be needed now. We've lost all of our heroes. Look how hungry we are for heroes."

"I can't lie to you and say that I saw all of this coming," I countered, the WRKO board ops probably perplexed and mocking us with doodles while this organic and odd exchange took place, as they were in Boston connecting me in Connecticut with Beck in Texas. "We were doing Top 40 radio and cracking on each other all the time, and you'd say 'go and read a Spider-Man comic book.' It was one of your go-to's. And when I left *Captain America: Civil War* I remember thinking I've gotta email Beck. He's gotta see this movie. You were the first person I thought of. But I can't lie to you and say that I always knew they were going to bring all of these characters that I loved as a kid to the big screen and what an impact they'd have. And what messages they were going to hand to them."

"I remember," he admitted, "You'd be like, 'Glenn, these are the greatest stories, and my collection means the world' and I'd just blow them off as comic books. Because I didn't grow up with them. I started reading them with my son and now we go to the comic book store together and everything and I'm really into the comic book, I guess, culture. Because of my son. I mean, you couldn't make a movie like Marvel makes these movies, with those messages, and extol the virtues of everything that America has stood for . . . I don't know if the liberals in Hollywood know what they're really saying and doing. They're extolling everything that we stand for." Reminder: This was 2019.

"Sometimes, as the comic book geek that I am, I get ticked off," I added. "I watch award shows where they introduce Ryan Coogler as a man who created an extraordinary world—a place where the Black Panther dwells. And it's like, Stan Lee, an old Jewish man, created that world in 1966 and that fact can't get swept under a rug."

"Stan Lee was way ahead of his time. I think Stan Lee is as important as . . . imagine this, Vinnie, me saying this back to you in the '90s: I think Stan Lee is as important to the American image and how we view things now, as a culture, as Walt Disney was."

"I knew that's where you were going," I told him, as Beck was a huge Walt Disney fan during our time together, and I'd often hear him rave about the architect of "The House of the Mouse" on his show after mine would go off the air, though those raves would taper when Disney would get embroiled in its latest scandal or cave to the pressures of wokeism.

"Imagine an America without Walt Disney," he went on to say, in a tone that implied it'd be impossible. Or, at the very least, not something anyone in their right mind would ever want to. "It's not the same. Imagine an America without Captain America and all that Stan Lee did."

"I'll probably regret going here," I countered, "but I so dreaded the day that Stan Lee passed. And there were times that I'd read about Glenn Beck sitting with Bono somewhere and all these other icons, and when Stan passed I thought, 'Well, he never met Stan!' Is that twisted? Is that dark?"

"What if I told you that I had dinner with him?"

"No! Did you? Why did I jump to the conclusion that you hadn't? Did you really? Be truthful. You're known for your honesty."

"I'm just gonna leave it at . . . could be. Maybe I did, maybe I didn't."

"I don't wanna say son of a bitch on RKO because that might cost me getting back on here."

"No, don't do that. I will tell you the truth because I love you. I didn't, and when he died I really regretted that I hadn't ever."

Sticking to the transcript: "That's great news that you didn't. I do wanna thank you not only for calling in today but one time in the past few years you made a crack, because we're always breaking them off on each other: 'Ah, you never appreciated what I did for you.' The gift you gave me, of this industry, of this microphone, a world I didn't even know existed, it was like you pulled back a curtain on something, so if I never did thank you I'll take this opportunity to, on the favorite radio station of your youth, the House that Charlie Van Dyke built. Because a microphone has power and that was lost on me in the late '90s. And with great power comes great responsibility. In 2019 America this microphone's as good as a gun."

"It is. I will tell you, Vinnie, the best way to thank me? I'll give you exactly the words that a mentor gave me when I was sixteen. Actually, I was eighteen. He was a mentor of mine and I thanked him and he said, 'No. Don't thank me. Pass this on to someone else. Someone else that you think could have the same spark and then teach them everything that you know.' That's how you thank me."

"Like you did with me?"

"God, no!"

Cut to February 10, 2024. Early that morning I received a text from Glenn, who was back in Connecticut. He was still calling Texas home, had built a studio there, and formed a company there, Mercury Radio Arts.

His father-in-law, as previously mentioned, a towering figure in the community of Hamden, the very town Beck had lived his entire time with KC101 (despite that brief, catastrophic real estate venture in the neighboring town of Cheshire), the one where his wife had been born and raised, had just passed away. He had been hospitalized a week or so prior, the entire family rushing to be by his side. As such, Beck was doing his syndicated conservative radio show, for the first time ever, from the very building where his time as a Top 40 "shock jock" had come to an end.

He arrived not knowing how long he'd be in town for, but management was nonetheless eager to accommodate the now huge radio star, urging him to take over the studio of his choosing. He chose one far back in the now borderline-dilapidated building, what those in the biz would refer to as a production studio and, further, one that didn't even exist during the nine years he was on KC101.

He had been popping in on my show almost every day for the two weeks or so he wound up being in town, and we'd do breaks, running the gamut from subjects like how the theater kids in high school are no longer the sheepish, bullied lot depicted in John Hughes movies but instead roam the hallways like the mob, having gone from sopranos to *The Sopranos*, to then-President Biden's failing health and the fragile state of the country to us both now having a son and a daughter each, all swirling around the same ages, and the fear we felt about the America we were handing them. *Full throttle fusion.*

His text read exactly how one from Beck about such a thing would read, for those who know him well anyway, and even fervid listeners of his show, in a way only those who truly love the medium can. *The Glenn Beck Radio Program* was now heard on over 400 radio stations throughout the United States, plus there is the Sirius XM channel that airs it and Beck's Blaze TV, should anyone not be able to get enough of the guy. Many cannot.

His father-in-law's passing was "beautiful," he wrote. His time had been a long one coming and Beck found watching this sizable Italian-American family locking hands around a hospital bed, alternately laughing and crying, each armed with their own personal goodbye, a sight to behold. He'd even gotten his own and referred to it as a "gift." While many of us often view the passing of a patriarch as criminal, as him being "taken" from us, here was Beck seeing it as him leaving. "He wasn't taken, Vinnie," he'd in fact tell me later that day, his voice awash in the same certainty and incredulousness that fuel so many of his sprawling, pause-laden radio monologues. "He *left*. He was done."

The laughing and crying continued that very night, mere hours later, with only the immediate family, Tania's best friend since high school, and myself, all wrapped around several tables crammed together at Encore by Goodfellas, old pal Gerry's very popular restaurant in downtown New Haven. Heavy on the former, I ribbed Beck much like I did those few years we'd worked together during the late 1990s, where Beck was often chastised by management for playing too few songs an hour, and when he did, punctuated doing so by mocking the artists. (Incidentally, I'll never forget the day some rando said to me, "With Glenn gone we can finally play more than three songs an hour." I quickly clarified that we were good for four and that four songs an hour felt like the right amount, only to not leave well enough alone and ask how many we were not only expected it to be playing all those years but now would be. And the answer was eleven.)

Then they brought out the cake and we all sang "Happy Birthday" to Glenn. The day his father-in-law *left* doubled as Beck's sixtieth birthday.

Encore by Goodfellas was easily Gerry's biggest restaurant yet, in the heart of New Haven. Iannacone, now a social media sensation getting likes from Emeril "Bam" Lagase himself, catered this last-minute birthday party as if it were a wedding with two hundred guests attending. The food just kept coming. But no bill ever did.

Beck struggled with the meal being on the house. It got to the point where he and Gerry had a stare-down, like two gunslingers in the Old West. Beads of sweat may've formed on their respective foreheads, I'm not sure. The tiramisu, espresso, and Sambuca was flying for ol'VP. A hush fell over the entire table, every word they had to say on the matter having been said, a "who'll break first" if ever there was one. It took Beck's mother-in-law—a woman whose husband's passing had kicked off the day—saying simply, "Glenn, let him," for the issue to be resolved. Tip included.

Fact was, Iannacone felt indebted to Beck. *Feels* indebted to Beck. Plus, he's one of his biggest fans. As is Glenn one of his.

Glenn returned to Connecticut later in the year, at Thanksgiving, and Gerry took us in once more, albeit a considerably smaller gathering. I spent much of the evening chatting with Beck's only son, Raphe, whose penchant for sarcasm and love of history rivals his father's. We swapped cell phone numbers and Tony Robbins stories, and at one point, as the evening waned, I caught Glenn watching us out of the corner of his eye.

We had met while Beck was coming off an ugly divorce, only two of his four children born yet, and me still in my childhood bedroom, with various guests coming and going. Here we were a quarter of a century later and I was the one coming off an ugly divorce, with two children of my own, and Glenn having added two more to his litter. I watched him take in the scene: His former co-host, who he'd initially deemed a talented writer and "natural" (his word!) broadcaster, who'd gotten swept up in the undertow of local radio "fame," washed out to sea with drink and women and notoriety. He warned me early on about what he called "velvet handcuffs." Cautioned me not to put them on, no matter how tempting it would be to do so, especially in the town I was born and raised in. Faith was in the room, threw me a wink, nodded that I should go ahead and do it. As if I needed her blessing. They didn't get put on me. I ordered those suckers, picked out the color. Glenn viewed my potential as having been eclipsed by *big fish, small pond-itis*. At one point he may've even felt like he doomed me.

But here he was watching the remnants of that '90s wild child engaging with his son, every bit the father he'd been for twice as long. He reconciled with the simple fact that despite goals and ambition I couldn't quite corral, I too had found my way onto the talk radio dial, doing "The Vinnie Penn Project," and had found my own tiny little way.

Yeah, I had stuck with the writing, and even had a few books published, every one of which I stand by. (No need to go seeking them out, as I'll never see a penny in royalties and most of them were deals with tiny boutique houses that no longer even exist, making it a largely futile endeavor; a childhood friend who moved away long ago did find a signed copy of one of my books on Amazon and confided that it was actually signed to my godmother! Its days as a coaster in my aunt's house had clearly run out! There *is* a zombie book I wrote, I must say, that's very cool.)

I did score the big New York agent at one point and he did shop the big labor of love of mine, but to no avail. More name-dropping: I drank a night away arm-in-arm in New Haven with the since-passed Elizabeth Wurtzel, author of best-seller *Prozac Nation*, wherein we bemoaned the drudgery of trotting our wares, the false starts and screeching halts in the biz, celebratory agent lunches wherein there isn't anything necessarily being celebrated, and that night we may've even grazed magic. It rhymes with tragic for a reason.

As for my radio show, that's some full circle shit. It began in 2010 at WELI, in the very studio where I did my first ever radio break. I was contacted by Clear Channel and asked if I'd be interested in returning to the local airwaves. With those aforementioned books having such an aversion to bestseller lists, I eagerly accepted, now a father of two, marriage in a state of decay, money playing its usual role in both that and my overenthusiastic yes to a new operations manager, freshly hired into New Haven by way of Atlanta. He had heard my demo. I was sure they were going to plug me in to the classic rock station in the cluster. When we met and he uttered the words "news/talk" I did a double take. "You want *me* to talk politics?" I sought to clarify. "Just do what you were doing for the company when you were on with Glenn," came the reply. Ya know, fusing.

Clear Channel was rebranded in 2014, much like I had been upon launching "The Project" four years earlier, becoming iHeart Radio. My show added Hartford's 1410/WPOP for simulcast the following year, and by 2020 "The Project" was also farmed out to iHeart stations like WTAG in Worcester, Massachusetts, and WRKO for a time. It's rinky-dink, but it's *my* rinky-dink. Local radio is important. Vital to the communities they serve. *Big fish, small pond-itis* notwithstanding.

Anyway, Glenn leaned in, clearly taken aback, observing, "You two have been talking nonstop for half the dinner like no one else is even here." Raphe fired back the kind of shot only a smartass son can.

It wasn't until later, at home, sharing all of this with my daughter, who had joined us on that first visit to Encore earlier in the year, wherein I recall looking at her speaking with Glenn, probably with the *identical* expression on my face, that it dawned on me that his swell of curiosity and pride could have just as easily been curated by Raphe. In fact, it was my daughter who pointed that very real possibility out.

But I don't think so.

It was three years of crazy. Nineties crazy. For me it was a raucous, oftentimes debaucherous, oftentimes Ecstasy-fueled three-year *party* (where Glenn occasionally played The Pooper), and for Glenn it was a three-year road to reinvention. It was a key chapter in both of our lives. That dinner in 2024 served as a reminder of that to Beck, who'd no doubt spent the past quarter of a century looking back on those years as transformative only for me. He'd been too distressed during them to even register his reinvention. Even while he was commandeering it. Manifesting all that was to come.

He sat in that restaurant, surrounded by friends and family from those three years either directly or indirectly, reflecting on them, with their high highs and low lows, looking across a table to truly register he'd found the woman who saved his life in this place and sitting beside her was the co-host who eventually drove him so to the brink of madness it confirmed his suspicions that his Top 40 years were over.

The next day I woke to this text from Beck: "We really did have fun way back when, didn't we?"

To which I replied, "It was the fusion of entertainment and enlightenment."

I don't know if Glenn agrees with that or even understood what I was saying. We wouldn't text each other again for several months, and it would be me initiating to discuss writing what you're holding in your hands right this instant. Glenn's show now is ultimately not very different than the show we did in the late '90s, in my opinion. He's just not back-selling Justin Bieber (thank God; although Glenn doing dramatic readings of Beebs's hits would be hysterical, and I believe he still does the occasional dramatic reading of lyrics on occasion, further illustrating my point). Glenn was fusing entertainment and enlightenment *when I met him*—he just didn't know it.

Beck was, for my money anyway, a talk show host the *entirety* of our time together, and went on to become a Marconi Award–winning member of the Radio Hall of Fame and host of one of the most popular talk shows in the country. *He's* the titular two talk show hosts. I hope you didn't think I was referring to moi there!?

I once declared in the KC101 studio—apropos of nothing—while a song was playing and we plundered egg sandwiches, "The one who cares least wins." Glenn stopped eating, placing his sandwich down, mulling this over, but I could by this point already read his face: He vehemently disagreed. Even so, he nonetheless allowed this off-the-cuff remark, this quip, this hangover-generated wannabe bumper sticker during the wasteland years between bumper stickers and memes, between T-shirt proclamations and Pinterest, to marinate.

"I don't like that at all," he finally said.

"What I mean," I began, but his hand came up quick, which I could read by now too.

"Tut tut," he managed, hoisting his sandwich back up, a good portion of the song left to go. "Save it for the air."

Always save it for the air.